Turnaround Strategies

for Customer Centric Operations

Turn-by-Turn Directions on the Path to Recovery

Jack Skinner

ITALICS PUBLISHING

Limitation of Liability/Disclaimer of Warranty
This book contains the author's opinions and advice regarding the subject matter of the book. Please take note that such advice may not be suitable to your particular situation. You should, therefore, seek the advice of a professional for your particular situation.

The contents of the book are based on the author's research, experience, and education, and the author has been diligent in the preparation and writing of this book.

The content and all materials contained herein are provided on an "as is" basis. The author does not make any guarantees or warranties of any kind, either express or implied, including, but not limited to, adequacy, accuracy, currentness, completeness or performance of, or results to be obtained from accessing and using the content of the book.

The author specifically disclaims any expressed or implied warranty of merchantability or fitness for a particular purpose relative to the contents of the book or the advice given therein. No warranty may be created by any representative of the author or by written sales material. The author shall not be liable to the reader, user, or anyone else for any inaccuracy, delay, interruption in service, error or omission, regardless of cause, or for any damages resulting therefrom, including but not limited to any loss of profit, consequential or special damages, costs, expenses or any other damages relative to the contents of this book.

Italics Publishing Inc.
Editor: Joni Wilson
Cover and interior design by Sam Roman and Adina Cucicov
Front cover image © tiero—Fotolia.com. Used by permission.
ISBN: 1-945302-17-8
ISBN-13: 978-1-945302-17-6

For Sam,

for so many reasons.

Author's Note

The examples and case studies given in this book are inserted to help illustrate concepts. They do not identify actual companies or individuals. All recognizable features were created and pieced together to exemplify hypothetical cases. All corporate and individual names are fictional, and there is no correlation among these fictional—corporate and individual—names and any real companies or individuals. Any resemblance of an example, case study, product, service, situation, or character, to any actual individuals or facts is entirely coincidental.

Contents

Author's Note 5
Contents 7
Introduction 9
Chapter 1 What Is Corporate Turnaround? 11
Chapter 2 Turnaround Consultants and Their Role 13
Stage 1 Assessment, Planning, and Pre-Work 17
Chapter 3 Initial Assessment: How Bad Is It? Do We Know What Is Broken? 18
Chapter 4 Plan Your Strategy for the Little Time You Have 23
Chapter 5 Key Leadership Education and Alignment 30
Chapter 6 Building Blocks for Driving Performance 35
Chapter 7 Internal Strategic Alliances 42
Chapter 8 Voice of Employees 46
Chapter 9 Recruiting the Players for the Turnaround Team 55
Chapter 10 Corporate Culture Evaluation 59
Chapter 11 No Taboos 67
Chapter 12 Voice of Customer 70
Chapter 13 Who Is in Charge? 82
Chapter 14 Documentation Planning 86
Chapter 15 Meetings Management 93
Chapter 16 Internal Communication 98
Stage 2 Execution 104
Chapter 17 Right-Sizing the Organization 105
Chapter 18 Executing Layoffs 117

Chapter 19 Accurate Revenue Forecasting 126
Chapter 20 Variable versus Fixed in Volatile Sales Environments 134
Chapter 21 Note on Decision Making 138
Chapter 22 Focus on Quality 143
Chapter 23 Notes on Strategic Sourcing 146
Chapter 24 The Right Metrics 151
Chapter 25 Goals and Objectives—Setting and Alignment 155
Chapter 26 Performance Reviews 166
Chapter 27 Bonus Program 174
Chapter 28 Cross-Functional Visibility: Scorecards and Dashboards .. 183
Chapter 29 Optimized Organizational Design 188
Stage 3 Stabilization 193
Chapter 30 Wrapping Up a Successful Turnaround 194
Chapter 31 Stabilization and Control 201
Chapter 32 Developing a Long-Term, Customer-Centric Strategy 206
Chapter 33 Conclusion 213
Final Note 215
About the Author 216
Bibliography 217

Introduction

"Always bear in mind that your own resolution to succeed is more important than any one thing."

~Abraham Lincoln (1809–1865)

Chapter 1
What Is Corporate Turnaround?

Corporate turnaround is the set of actions and strategies applied to reverse a company's descending trajectory: from free fall into the depths of financial distress, back up toward profitability and growth.

If your company is merely not making enough money, has a slow growth rate or had a somewhat bad year, a more relaxed, yet equally resolute transformation action might be more appropriate. Turnarounds are reserved for those who are in need of decisive, immediate action to ensure the company's survival in the following twelve months.

Going back to the basics, there are three main reasons a company is losing money:

- Sales revenue is too low.
- Operating expenses are too high.
- A combination of the above.

This book focuses on the challenging realm of operational turnarounds. While it does not aim to cover everything there is to know about this topic, it proposes turnaround strategies that can yield immediate results without sacrificing the customer experience, or jeopardizing sales, growth, or stability. The operational sphere is usually the one carrying the largest price tag and causing the steepest loss. While sales revenue cannot be increased beyond a certain level, or, in times of recession sales volume will remain volatile and constantly underperforming, an operational turnaround is the strategy that saves the company and positions it for future growth. This book will not analyze bankruptcy options, debt-restructuring alternatives, or recommend sourcing strategies—with a few minor exceptions. We will maintain our focus on operations and, of course, on the customer.

The first victim in times of trouble is the customer. Sometimes, decision makers at the helm of troubled companies decide to cut costs in areas that impact negatively the customers and their decisions to purchase, further pushing the company revenue down the drain. Although saluted as cost-cutting alternatives, which "save our jobs and our future," these initiatives end up being proven wrong by history in a dramatic way. All these decision makers have one thing in common: they do not know their customers; they don't understand the drivers behind the customers' decisions to purchase.

The difference between a successful and an unsuccessful operational turnaround is the ability to carefully balance the priorities between the financial constraints of the troubled company and its customers' best interest. This is a thin line to walk, as for the successful execution of an operational turnaround, there is limited time and little, if any, room for error. The long-term success of any turnaround depends on its stability. This, in turn, depends on the customers, and on the customers' willingness to remain loyal, refer, or further engage with the company. Therefore, part of ensuring the stabilization of any operation is a deep understanding of the customers' needs, wants, satisfiers, and dissatisfiers, and the impact we make on every interaction with the customers. Are we able to address their needs better, more affordably, and in a more attractive manner than the competition? Do we know, understand, and respect our customers? Are we keeping track of how our customers are changing, evolving with the times, how they are altering their purchasing habits and their tastes for different products and services? Can we keep up with it all?

One of the most difficult things for troubled company leaders is to accept there's an operational problem they can't fix. The problem continues to exist despite their best efforts to address it; it's a problem that eludes them somehow, and causes them losses of time, money, and restful sleep. They've thrown money and resources at this problem, challenged the best and brightest internal resources with it, all in vain. Accepting the existence of such a problem, though difficult, is the first step toward resolving it. What makes it so difficult is that the problem can't be easily defined; sometimes the best way to put it is, "We're losing money and we don't know how to contain it; we don't know how to stop that." That's where it all starts.

Chapter 2
Turnaround Consultants and Their Role

A key element of the successful operational turnaround is the turnaround consultant.

No one in the current leadership structure of the organization can win this battle without help; they had their chance to fix things and they have failed. The current recipe—consisting of human resources, policies, standard operating procedures, corporate culture, etc.—has failed.

Not everything in this bowl of soup is bad, though. The *combination* of these components and the way they interact has been proven to be a failure, through undisputable results. In some cases, the failure was caused by the proverbial closeness to the trees, impeding the leader to see any bit of the forest.

For the operational turnaround consultant, there is no closeness. There are no ties to the company's culture or history, getting in the way of critical measures in need of implementation. There are no preconceived notions of what the customers might or might not like about company ABC's products and services. The worker who belongs on the layoff list is not the consultant's old college buddy, and they've never had a beer together; there is no bias.

With a turnaround consultant, there is no emotion behind business decisions. The decisions are made through a data-driven, emotionless, formal decision-making process, geared at yielding the best results possible in the briefest time. The operational consultant brings a fresh pair of eyes and can spot "black holes" without any hesitation. These "black holes," present in many failing operational environments, are ways of doing things or operating procedures that bleed cash without a clear, documented benefit. They are enduring relics of an obsolete, maladaptive culture that no longer belongs.

Case Study

Emily, customer service project manager, was reviewing warranty data for the core line of products and had noticed an inconsistency between overall defects reported for the core line in the zero-to-three year product age group and the number of tent flies shipped for the same product range. After inquiring about this, she received the following explanation:

"It's the one-time-only fly replacement policy," the head of Customer Operations had said.

"How do you mean?" Emily asked.

"Well, if our customers call in and ask for a second tent fly, a different color maybe, or a different weather class, we'd ship it to them. One time only for each customer."

"For free?" Emily asked, eyes round in disbelief.

"Absolutely, we've always done it like that," John concluded.

"Well, we need to change that; we can't continue giving stuff away for free," Emily sighed. "I'll put together a recommendation for a policy change," she added.

"You will do no such thing," John snapped. "This has been our tradition with our customers for 15 years. We have different things to focus on."

This example illustrates a black hole's sacred existence, despite the fact that some employees do find it, challenge it for valid business reasons, and yet fail when attempting to drive the change, in the fight against company culture and outdated tradition. Change is tough.

The operational turnaround consultant is the ultimate change agent; has experience implementing unpopular, against-the-grain changes; and is focused on immediate, attainable financial results. Using the example about Emily and John, the fact that the one-time-only fly replacement policy has been in place for 15 years is no argument; this policy would have to go, immediately. The outsider is safe from cultural contamination or pressures.

There is great value in securing the help of a good operational turnaround leader, who brings a global vision, with experience in implementing aggressive fixes that have been proven to work in other corporations. Rather than having multiple projects aimed at improving policy and process, the overall view of the turnaround leader or consultant will remove the "patching the patch" strategy encountered in many failing operational environments. Bringing a systemic approach, the fixes are aimed to redesign the operational structure rather than apply a quick patch that will not last long.

The consultant will be able to adjust this approach based on specifics of the business and design the operational organization with flexibility and variability in mind. Another key quality of the turnaround consultant is true out-of-the box thinking. Although many of us think we are—and are surrounded with—out-of-the-box thinkers, this is not entirely true, not to its full extent. Corporate culture and its forms of pressure can build one wall for the thinking box. Peer pressure could build another. Fears about job security, advancement, performance reviews, bonus and/or merit increase eligibility, could apply significant censorship to the internal employee's out-of-the-box thinking ability.

In most cases, true out-of-the-box thinkers who are troubled by such fears will still think the solutions, but hesitate in driving the implementation of such solutions, especially those based on dramatic shifts from traditional, established, and "safe-for-my-career" ways to do business. These internally employed out-of-the-box thinkers can be engaged in becoming valuable resources in the turnaround process.

The success of an operational turnaround highly depends on the company's resolve. You, as the CEO, have decided you need help to turn your company around. That's the first step. Once the consultant comes in and starts working, there will be many loud voices in the leadership resisting parts of the drastic change. The changes would take some leaders out of their comfort zones; in some cases expose their failures. They will feel invaded, their egos bruised, and their toes stepped on. They will hide behind arguments such as company culture, tradition, and "our own way" to do things.

Although initially on board with the turnaround initiative, once they see how it affects their areas, they will hesitate and push back. Sometimes the push back will be inconspicuous, carefully disguised under a passive-aggressive willingness to cooperate. This is where your leadership resolve comes in handy. The consultant cannot force a company to turn around; the company has to want to survive, to fight for its life, and to embrace change.

You, as CEO, must assist in overcoming the defensive voice of these leaders, constantly get their buy-in, and let the results speak. Within two to three months, the first financial results will start showing and that means your turnaround efforts are on the right track. Consequently, that resistance will fade, quickly replaced by strong, heartfelt buy-in.

How long do you have to endure? An operational turnaround can take between six and twelve months, or more, depending on the size of the operation and the root causes for failure. Within the first 60 days after the work starts, you will be able to see the first financial results. A slower descent, maybe even a zero loss for the business unit can be achieved in as little as two to three months.

Since time is money and you're in a hurry, let's explore together the turnaround strategies most proven to be effective in customer centric operations.

Stage 1
Assessment, Planning, and Pre-Work

"A goal without a plan is just a wish."

~Antoine de Saint-Exupéry (1900–1944)

Chapter 3
Initial Assessment: How Bad Is It? Do We Know What Is Broken?

There are few signs outside the profit and loss (P&L) report to show that a company is struggling. The parking lot is full, people look busy, and they usually are. At first glance, you think everything is fine. Therefore, how can you tell what's wrong and how severe the problem might be? Finance will tell you which P&L lines are out of control, or much worse compared to last year. Linking this information to the corresponding faulty operational process is what will help you start fixing what's broken.

This diagnosis is not an easy one, especially with well-established companies that have grown during the past 25 years from small to medium to large. During their growth, most of the processes have been adjusted on the fly, without measured benefits and a documentation attached to them. Some companies started as a family-owned business and some of that family environment still exists, despite their initial public offering (IPO). It continues to exist, complete with tolerance for errors and treating every case as an exception to the rule. In short, it's chaos.

Before you can start working to make repairs, two initial questions need to be answered: how bad is the crisis, and how can you find what is broken. Let's find answers to these questions, one by one.

The first is answered quite easily by the answer to the following question, "If no action is taken to fix any issues, and we continue operating as we have so far, how much longer can we be in business?" This question bears a cash-flow answer. Since the answer is critically important to survival, it must be given in a conservative way. Do not assume your customers will suddenly decide to purchase twice the volume of last month. Do not plan to stop paying your vendors so you can make payroll.

A correct estimate requires you to continue to operate as you normally do: no extra borrowing, no aging payables. There's no reason to hope the economy will get better overnight; neither is there reason to hope that vendors will dramatically drop their prices. Quite the opposite—the glooming economy might further impact your customers' decision to purchase, banks might raise interest rates, and someone might sue you; so you should provision for those situations in your estimate. This is the time for cautious pessimism; better to be safe than sorry.

If the answer to how long you can remain in business indicates a period of six months or less, you need a miracle; you've waited too long and this is your "oh, crap!" moment of realization. The company can still be turned around, if the action is swift and the resolve is solid. When you have less than six months operating capabilities, there is no time for hesitation. Your turnaround consultant will recommend various strategies, depending on the time you have left. There is a need for immediate, decisive action, quick yet solid decision making, and even faster implementation of those decisions. This is not the time for the deer-in-the-headlights type of freeze.

If the answer shows you have more than six months, well, the greater the timeframe, the better options you have. You cannot relax though; your company is still losing money. The time for action is now. Some leaders will keep praying for a change of luck and wait for each month's financial results, holding their breaths, thus later becoming those with less than six months of survival left.

There's no point in waiting; unless there is dramatic turnaround action taken, what has failed in the recent past will continue to fail in the future, at a steeper pace each month. The company will be sliding on the downward spiral created by increasing debt, interest rates, decreasing customer confidence, tarnished reputation on the markets, panicked reactions, and discouraged, scared employees looking for work elsewhere. The best workers will leave first.

Now that the first question is out of the way, it's time to answer the second question: how can you find out what is broken in your business? Thankfully, there are three valuable sources of information: employees, suppliers, and customers.

The employees, if asked the right questions under an absolute guarantee of confidentiality and no reprisal, will gladly share what they see is wrong. After all, it's their jobs and they'd like to keep them, so they have a firsthand interest in the survival of the company. They are also closer to various operational aspects; this closeness and their individual experiences with the way processes have changed will give valuable insight into operational malfunctions or broken processes. Furthermore, the front-line workers, the customer-facing roles, will be able to provide insight into the way customers perceive company policies and how that perception influences their decisions to purchase and their customer loyalty.

More details will be given about capturing the voice of the employees in Chapter 8.

Suppliers can provide information in two ways: if surveyed with the right set of open-ended questions, they will indicate what makes the relationship difficult, where they struggle, where they see risks—quality, delivery times, etc.—and why. They will provide insight into how other companies use their products or services, or where they could see improvement in your process or the overall client–supplier relationship. The second way is to ask suppliers for solutions rather than products: for example, instead of "We need 450,000 cardboard boxes a year, this size," you could ask vendors to "Please provide us with a variety of packaging solutions, allowing us to ship 450,000 books a year, this size." It makes a world of difference, but there's a catch: this cannot turn into a spending spree. Good judgment must be used when selecting solutions proposed by vendors.

Case Study

Ted, account executive with Square Boxes Inc., a relatively large packaging company, was visiting one of his biggest accounts for the yearly renewal of the contract. The client, a consumer electronics manufacturer, was unhappy with the packaging company's products. He claimed that faulty packaging had led to numerous returns due to the product arriving broken or scratched. Ted had repeatedly assured the client that the products

were high quality and that such complaints were unique to this particular electronics manufacturer. He did not seem to convince the client though, so he decided to visit the client's assembly plant, with special attention given to the packaging area.
"This is where we package items, and, as you can see, we use the materials correctly. We inspect each box manually, and we don't cheap out on the Styrofoam shock absorbers," David, the warehouse manager said in an inpatient manner.

David was sick of it all. Every month he had been put through hell by his supervisor, the VP of Operations, because of the high rates of returns on LCD flat panels and plasma-screen TVs, due to scratches on the flat-panel surfaces. The plant's output quality was incredibly high, yet these returns were truly damaged. It must have been the packaging; no other reason would make sense. Over time, David had increased the amount of Styrofoam shock absorbers—also known as peanuts—and now the TVs were being shipped surrounded by them, without any major improvement being recorded in the product's quality-driven rate of return.

Ted was walking through the packaging area, watching TVs being covered in a protective sheet of polyethylene, fitted with protective foam at both ends, and then introduced into the box. After which point the worker filled the box with Styrofoam peanuts and slid the package containing the remote, a set of RCA cables, two batteries, and the user guide, in front of the TV's LCD panel, along the box wall.
"This is how you ship the accessories?" Ted asked, plunging his hand into the box and retrieving the package.
"Yes," David replied, brow rising.
"Well, that's your problem. This accessory package is loose inside the box. It has protrusions due to the batteries and the remote. It's heavier than the Styrofoam and, during shipping, it will find its way to the front panel, hitting it and scratching it. I bet that if we design a special slot in the side protectors, a place where the accessory package is immobilized safely, you could drop all your Styrofoam peanuts usage from these boxes. What do you think? Wanna give it a try?" Ted looked to David for a reaction.
David was smiling, for the first time in months.

The example above illustrates the fact that there is great benefit in allowing our suppliers to work with and for us. After all, who knows packaging better that a packaging manufacturer? By asking the supplier to provide an array of options, you can securely decide which price range makes sense for the current, financially challenged state of the business. This practice should not replace due diligence with suppliers, negotiating terms, or revisiting the issue every year.

Every year, vendor companies make progress: better materials, increased efficiencies reflected in lower pricing, different concepts, and improved design. Engaging vendors in our diagnosis efforts can help us pick up where we have fallen behind; technology and materials are evolving at an incredible rate and falling behind happens in every company, in every field, in every area, despite best efforts. Falling behind, however, comes with a hidden price tag that we cannot afford: losing our competitive edge. Having a rigorous, annual process of vendor selection and engagement in solutions design, can ensure we keep on track with the best on the market. Our customers are a valuable source of information as to what goes wrong in our business.

Chapter 12 is focused on the customers and their perceptions of our business, products, services, and overall interaction with our company.

The diagnosis phase of the operational turnaround is a critical one, yet the challenge is increased by the fact that it cannot take a long time. No matter how narrow the timeframe, if the issue is unknown, then it cannot be fixed. The following chapter looks into making the best use of the little time you have for the turnaround to be effective.

Chapter 4
Plan Your Strategy for the Little Time You Have

Whenever there's a strict deadline or time constraint on a complex project, task management plays a major role in the end result. Operational turnaround is no exception. All turnaround initiatives end up being executed under severe time constraints due to their nature. Therefore, the following three key elements make the difference between turnaround success and failure: task prioritization, tracking, and process ownership.

1. Task Prioritization

Selecting what would make the most difference in the shortest time is not a simple process. There are many factors to consider when making these decisions: financial benefit in the short and long term; cost associated with the change; impact on the customer; resources involved; legal, media, and public relations risks; operational viability; and so on. This is a complex problem with more than one solution.

One way to lay down a restructuring plan is to completely redesign the organization, followed by a transition map: from current state to future. To better illustrate this methodology, let's use an example: EXPL Inc. has posted gains in the recent few years; two years ago it posted $35M net profit, with sales revenue of $973M. However, last year it posted a loss of $37M, with sales revenue of $550M. For this year, the forecasts show a much steeper decline in sales, down to $396M. Unless significant action is taken, the company will run out of cash in a little over six months. EXPL Inc. is in the car sales business, with 38 dealerships nationwide. The industry is in a lot of trouble, and forecasts are grim.

Instead of spending inexistent time to sift through tons of data and reports, searching for elusive cost savings, the turnaround consultant will work with the senior leadership and design a business from ground up, for a forecast of $396M in sales. Let's call the future business EXPL 2. What would such a business need to have to be able to operate? How would it look? Let's think of an organization chart—no names, just functions for now.

In some cases, it is helpful to look back through the history of the respective company to the time when it used to be a $396M a year company—what did it look like then?

There's a caveat though—times change fast and consumers change with the times. There are major differences between the "now" and "back then" models: business channels or units that didn't exist or are no longer needed; efficiencies that were gained in the interim; new systems, processes, technologies, that have changed the core of the business; therefore, just applying the "back then" blueprint is risky. This method should be used with a lot of caution; as a ballpark indicator it can bring some insight though.

Redesigning the business from the ground up brings the opportunity for some interesting questions about need versus want, in addition to the company's core competencies. Especially in well-established businesses, some processes are traditionally done in-house, when in fact they should be outsourced, due to cost, time, and focus reasons. There goes the in-house printing services department (in charge of printing fliers and brochures for the dealerships), complete with manager, technicians, equipment, supplies, and all. A sourcing initiative that took 2.5 hours returned three local vendors with cycle times of 48 hours and under, with no contracts needed. Nope, EXPL Inc. does not have a competitive advantage in printing brochures; they should stick to selling cars.

A quick voice-of-customer exercise can be executed in a couple of days by asking dealership walk-ins who did not close a deal to provide some insight into their reasons not to purchase their next vehicle from EXPL Inc. This is a quick way to figure out which advertising, financing, warranty, and service programs are not working, and why. This can be taken one step forward, by asking what could help them change their minds, and gaining some more insight into consumer expectations, as they are being set by a variety of factors outside of your control: economy, competitor's advertising campaigns and promises, financing deals, perception of quality, comfort, and safety, and so on.

Competitive benchmarking is quite useful at this point. What are EXPL's competitors doing successfully? What worked for them and what didn't? Which competitor's car would we buy today, and why? A high-level view would be good enough due to the lack of time for in-depth analysis. This is how EXPL uncovers a surprising fact: their biggest competitor has an online sales division, generating sales four times the volume of their biggest dealership. Cost attached? No brick and mortar, no added inventory; just a few fast computers, somewhere at their headquarters, manned by some smart, ambitious, and well-compensated geeks, pushing vehicles through all channels: Autotrader.com, eBay, Yahoo Autos, social media, pay-per-click advertising. Everything is game.

Now the future EXPL is beginning to take shape. The organizational chart becomes clear; our design exercise is almost over. The time has come to build the transition map with action planning. This is the first high-level draft:

EXPL—Current Org	EXPL—Future Design	Key Actions
Headoffice overhead @ $12M	Headoffice overhead @ $4.9M	Reduce management headcount, redesign org, outsource backoffice functions
Dealership count: 38	Dealership count: 16	Identify low performing locations and close; reassign / liquidate inventory
-	Online sales division	Create, implement, staff
In-house printing operation	-	Outsource
Dealership level organization	Optimized, increased variability	Reduced fixed headcount, reassign tasks towards variable
Inventory $72 M	Inventory @ $30 M	Organize close-out sales events, heavy promo, sell at cost

Fig. 4.1. Turnaround action planning—transition map.

The analytics and reasoning behind the numbers chosen as targets are

based largely on right-sizing the structure to operate in profitability at the forecasted sales volume. The roadmap to the future operational structure is quite clear, complete with action items. We're ready to proceed.
In this chapter, we are focused on understanding prioritization, tracking, and process ownership.

Details about the analytics and the implementation strategy for this kind of plan will be discussed in Chapter 17.

2. Tracking

With so many balls in the air, there's an acute need for someone to watch and make sure two things happen:

- No balls will be dropped: no action will be forgotten, executed out of order, or delayed.
- There is clear communication among action item (tasks) owners. In most cases, the key action items in the turnaround plan are interconnected; no department can operate in complete isolation from the rest of the business.

The best way to ensure this level of execution is to think of the entire action plan in terms of a project, complete with project manager, task list, resource allocation, and Gantt chart.

The project manager for our turnaround project is more a central point of contact for all updates and a process-check person. He or she will be, most likely, a part of your turnaround consultant's own staff. He or she will be the one who can give the turnaround consultant an update at any given time on the status of execution, on completed items, delayed items, revised dates of completion, resource allocation issues, roadblocks, and bottlenecks. The project manager is the go-between and timekeeper for all leaders with key action items on their agendas.

Using the same EXPL high-level action plan illustrated above, this would be a snapshot of the project manager's view of it:

WBS	Name	Duration	Start	Finish
1	**Operational turnaround**	97 days	18-Feb	2-Jul
1.1	**Reduce head office overhead by 60%**	63 days	18-Feb	15-May
1.1.1	**Redesign organizational chart**	42 days	18-Feb	16-Apr
1.1.1.1	Identify key functions in new structure	28 days	18-Feb	27-Mar
1.1.1.2	Right size office support functions	14 days	30-Mar	16-Apr
1.1.2	**Outsource back office functions**	61 days	18-Feb	13-May
1.1.2.1	Identify outsourceable functions	28 days	18-Feb	27-Mar
1.1.2.2	Vendor selection, contracting, SLA	5 days	30-Mar	3-Apr
1.1.2.3	Transition	28 days	6-Apr	13-May
1.1.3	**Reduce management headcount**	21 days	17-Apr	15-May
1.1.3.1	Identify impacted staff	7 days	17-Apr	27-Apr
1.1.3.2	Execute layoff	14 days	28-Apr	15-May
1.2	**Reduce dealership count by 60%**	97 days	18-Feb	2-Jul
1.2.1	Identify low performing locations	28 days	18-Feb	27-Mar
1.2.2	Transfer, reassign or closeout inventory	30 days	30-Mar	8-May
1.2.3	Execute local layoffs	14 days	11-May	28-May
1.2.4	Negotiate location close, lease buyouts	30 days	30-Mar	8-May
1.2.5	Close selected locations	25 days	29-May	2-Jul
1.3	**Create online sales division**	20 days	18-Feb	17-Mar
1.3.1	Select staffing, hire, train	15 days	18-Feb	10-Mar
1.3.2	Install equipment	14 days	18-Feb	9-Mar
1.3.3	Develop guidelines, policies, etc.	14 days	18-Feb	9-Mar
1.3.4	Launch—marketing PR and media	5 days	11-Mar	17-Mar
1.4	**Close inhouse printing operation**	32 days	18-Feb	2-Apr
1.4.1	Vendor selection, contracting, SLA	2 days	18-Feb	19-Feb
1.4.2	Transition	14 days	20-Feb	11-Mar
1.4.3	Execute layoffs	14 days	12-Mar	31-Mar
1.4.4	Close department	2 days	1-Apr	2-Apr
1.5	**Dealership re-organization for remaining locations**	69 days	18-Feb	25-May
1.5.1	Optimize dealership org—increase variable cost	45 days	18-Feb	21-Apr
1.5.2	Execute layoffs	14 days	22-Apr	11-May
1.5.3	Implement new aggressive bonus structure	10 days	12-May	25-May
1.6	**Reduce inventory by 60%**	40 days	18-Feb	14-Apr
1.6.1	**Organize close-out sale events**	28 days	18-Feb	27-Mar
1.6.1.1	Establish aggressive promotional program	14 days	18-Feb	9-Mar
1.6.1.2	Launch new media creative in support of closeou	28 days	18-Feb	27-Mar
1.6.2	Reassign units to best selling locations	40 days	18-Feb	14-Apr

Fig. 4.2. Operational turnaround plan mapped in project management software.

Choosing good project management software is helpful for such a complex project. From this view, the turnaround consultant can monitor carefully the execution of the action plan, identify any resource allocation conflicts, and make sure the turnaround plan stays on track. The Gantt chart is a visual aid, identifying the critical path (the sequence of tasks that dictates the project finish date):

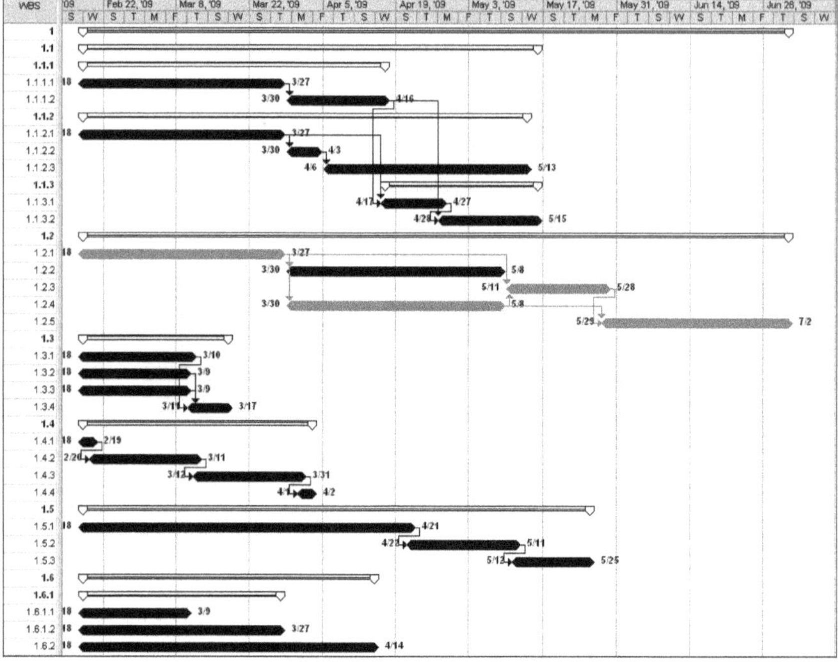

Fig. 4.3. Gantt chart view of operational turnaround plan, showing the critical path in gray.

There are a few important observations at this point:

- The duration entered for the tasks is for illustration purposes; similar tasks might take more or less time in different companies, depending on the company's specifics.
- However, the visual aid above—the Gantt chart—clearly illustrates that 11 different tasks can be started and executed simultaneously, therefore contributing to a fast execution of the operational turnaround plan.

3. Process Ownership

Each task contributing to the operational turnaround has to have an owner, to ensure the simultaneous execution (illustrated in Fig. 4.3.), the accountability and ownership of the actions taken, and a hierarchical structure associated with this execution. More specifically, a summary task's owner is also the leader of the team executing that particular summary task and its component subtasks. The success of this action plan depends greatly on the ownership and clear reporting structure of the key contributors. This is neither the time nor the place for dotted-line reporting structures, gray areas, or any other form of organizational design confusion.

Therefore, our example transition map now looks like this:

EXPL—Current Org	EXPL—Future Design	Key Actions	Owner(s)
Headoffice overhead @ $12M	Headoffice overhead @ $4.9M	Reduce management headcount, redesign org, outsource backoffice functions	Jones (Stevens, Corey, Smith, Johnson)
Dealership count: 38	Dealership count: 16	Identify low performing locations and close; reassign / liquidate inventory	Adams (Benson, Evans, McDonnel)
-	Online sales division	Create, implement, staff	Samuel (Jameson, Schmidt)
In-house printing operation	-	Outsource	Johnson
Dealership level organization	Optimized, increased variability	Reduced fixed headcount, reassign tasks towards variable	Matthews (Stevens, Foley)
Inventory $72M	Inventory @ $30M	Organize close-out sales events, heavy promo, sell at cost	Trenton (Peterson, Phelps, Ricks)
Project Manager: Chris Jackson (XYZ Consulting)			

Fig. 4.4. Turnaround action planning—transition map, with teams and PM.

A final note on task process ownership: any operational turnaround action in need of fast execution and immediate results needs to have an aggressive bonus plan attached to the milestones, with clear metrics and checkpoints in place, recognizing overachievement in a bold manner. By far this is more effective in driving exceptional results faster than any other of performance management. Motivating through rewards, and, more specifically, financial rewards, is what will help keep tasks on track and delivered on time and specs.

More on ownership and motivation will be discussed in Chapter 6, focused on driving performance.

Chapter 5
Key Leadership Education and Alignment

Key leadership, even if initially on board with the idea of a turnaround, will become hesitant as things move forward. There are two main root causes behind this fact, both stemming from normal human behavior: fear of change and defensive behavior. Your turnaround consultant will carefully manage both and accurately foresee them, as they are expensive and disruptive to ignore, but also quite common.

1. Fear of Change

Older than the ages, the biggest enemy of progress generates—in all environments— resistance, anguish, pain, and any other form of negative employee emotion or reaction you can think of. People will greet change—everywhere it might arrive—with the same vast array of weapons, armed and ready to fire: objections, threats, disruptions in routines, accusations, resignations, strikes, sabotage acts, etc. This will happen in all cases, for all changes—big and small—unless change comes accompanied by a change management process.

There are a few basic steps to any change management process. With most turnarounds, there is little time; therefore, change management cannot take too long either. These few easy steps will ensure a dramatic drop in resistance levels, for all kinds of change:

- **Communication.** Fear of change is, essentially, fear of the unknown. Turning the unknown into the less unknown directly diminishes the fear levels.

- **Start at the top, but trickle down fast.** There should be hierarchy in change management communication, one that goes hand-in-hand with the level of information confidentiality, as well as to what is important for the audience. "Audience" is the keyword in this paragraph; a good communication plan has to identify clearly the audiences and goals for each audience; timing is also important. What are you trying to communicate, to whom, why, and how often? What are the indicators for success?

- **Sell the change.** Argue it, explain the drivers, the need for change. Answer questions, address concerns, and make sure everyone is on board before considering it done. Be very clear with everyone stating the time for expressing concerns is now, part of the change management process, as opposed to later, as a form of resistance. Address and eliminate any political games that could take your change hostage and use it for hidden agendas. Set clear expectations openly; this will pay back tenfold.

- **Make it personal.** Explain what's at stake. Throw in a few bones, create ownership and implement performance recognition programs. Draw a clear picture of the rewards that come with the change; turn it into a positive message with individual benefits: what's in it for each and every one of your employees?

- **Eliminate cultural clashes.** Some changes will go against established company culture. This issue needs immediate clarification, because it can create chaos and confusion, as the old ways meet the new, revolutionary ways to tackle the same challenges. Company culture is often to blame for the downturn, at least in part, so it needs to also embrace change.

- **Contingency planning.** Have a contingency plan drawn out, a fallback plan in case something goes wrong. Keep it simple. Communicate it properly, train on it, and make sure it comes complete with the definitions of change success and failure, in addition to checkpoints at important milestones, established and with assigned owners.

2. Defensive Behavior

Anyone can get defensive under fire; that is normal, instinctive, and has helped our species survive and evolve to this day and age. It can also mean that the leader you are counting on for support with your turnaround action is suddenly irrational, sometimes hysterical. His chain of thought becomes erratic and his logic completely vanishes, leaving room for vengeful thoughts and lasting grudges.

So, if this is normal, how do we deal with it? The ability to defuse the players' defensive shields and missiles can make the difference between success and failure in a turnaround. The key is going after the trigger to the defensive behavior—the perceived threat.

For example, the simple mentioning of a department name when analyzing causes behind a quarterly loss will make the department head defensive. After all, his performance is under attack. His methods are under fire, his credibility questioned without an opportunity for self-defense, he will be hung out to dry—that's for sure. He will be publicly embarrassed, in front of his snickering enemies and ungrateful direct reports. He is now finished. He should be going straight home, to update his résumé and start looking for work elsewhere. He did not belong here anyway . . . he had told the CEO only eight months ago that he needed to change things around, and he wasn't allowed to make those changes. Now they're crucifying him . . . he needs to get going. He needs a stiff drink.

Amazing . . . All this anguish from a simple listing of a department name on a turnaround cost reduction plan, drafted and presented for the first time on a PowerPoint slide. Not even a conversation on the subject has taken place. By the time someone approaches this department head, he will have plunged straight into irrational land, and good luck making any progress. That is, if he's still around.

As with fear of change, there are a few steps to follow in preventing the triggering of defensive behaviors. Unlike fear of change though, these steps are far from basic; they are a challenging balancing act and they require skill and native talent.

- **Define threats.** This is almost never a documented step; the majority of experienced and talented leaders have a sense for what others could perceive as threatening. Because turnarounds are extreme from this perspective, a little bit more thinking should happen around threats and threatened areas, or leaders who might feel threatened. Who and what they are, who they are impacting, how to best communicate, how to mitigate the associated risks. This is not the time and place to forget companies are made of people; feelings drive people to act, and no process can ever supersede that. However, other feelings can compensate and turn everything to positive action.

➢ **Prioritize threats.** What is scarier: being one of the leaders who need to embrace change so they can turn their departments around? Or having the company file for Chapter 7? The answer could be surprising. Egos are powerful; this change coming their way makes some people feel like failures, exposed, insecure, humiliated, etc. Therefore, some would take Chapter 7 over that with little hesitation; secretly, of course, and instinctively. It wouldn't be about "me" anymore; it would become about "us," and there is instinctual safety in that. No one will ever state that out loud, but sometimes actions are supporting this conclusion. Getting the leaders out of this state of mind requires getting their bruised egos out of the way. Ask them to think what they would do if this was their company. Spell out for them the benefits of change, as in personal and financial, performance related. The biggest motivators for this social group (leadership) are money and prestige: offer both as rewards, aggressively.

➢ **Do not use force.** Telling a defensive leader to "stop being defensive or there will be consequences" is one of the most pathetic forms of aggravating an employee ever encountered. It's also a complete waste of time. Unfortunately, it is also one of the most often encountered methods of so-called bringing defensive behavior to order. If we remember that defensive behavior is instinctive, the key is to not engage the defensive person. We should resist the urge to argue, press, and corner him. Let him cool down on his own, before saying harsh things and burning any bridges. Then address his objections and ask direct questions; empathize with him. Sometimes it is fruitful to have an open conversation probing the reasons behind the defensive behavior and exploring the root causes. If someone feels threatened, maybe it's worth our time to figure out why, because of the obvious performance and decision-making consequences of these feelings. Of course, this is a conversation that needs to happen after we are well restored to logic land—after the employee's instinctive defensiveness has subsided and has been replaced by logical, frontal-lobe thought processes.

➢ **Turn threats into goals and establish metrics for them.** Goals are something a leader can deal with—easily. He will even enjoy it, if there's a hefty reward in sight. Therefore, if a systems change is the initial threat, implementing the new system can become a goal, which pays 25 percent bonus after completion with zero business disruption and zero delay. Your foe has become your motivated friend.

➢ **Restore leaders' confidence.** After this emotional journey taking leaders from threatened/defensive to engaged/productive, we should do one more thing: restore their confidence. Some will still blame themselves—or others—for the company's crisis, and dwell on real or imaginary mistakes of the past. Steer them gently toward the future and ask them to focus on their team members—who need their leaders' support as they struggle with change—and on their goals—which will lead to the comeback. Repeat this message as often as you need.

➢ **Face reality**. Sadly, some will not cut it in the new world. They could be too negative, too political, or too rigid. They might decide to remain part of the problem rather than become a part of the solution. They could be strong believers in a company culture that belongs in the past. They are the hallway politicians and feared backstabbers so well known in every company facing hardship. They are preoccupied solely with positioning themselves and with looking good. They are concerned only with what they can make happen for themselves today, with little or no concern for long-term stability and viability. For any number of reasons, some will simply not make it. Failing to recognize them in time or failing to deal with them promptly will generate roadblocks of all kinds. They deserve good severance, just like the rest of the laid-off workforce; it was not their fault; they are a product of a malfunctioning environment.

With these two main points in mind, getting buy-in from most leaders becomes feasible in just a little time, provided it is accompanied by clear goals and enticing rewards. Most important, the buy-in would be real, not just a front put on by pressured, defensive leaders, fearing for their jobs and looking for ways out. It is the true buy-in, heart and soul, combined with achievable rewards, which will generate the creative, impactful, and immediate results needed to reverse the fall.

Chapter 6
Building Blocks for Driving Performance

In the complex execution of a turnaround plan, driving performance can constitute a challenge. Focus might shift numerous times; pressures from various directions could cause conflicting agendas to collide, and so on.

Case Study

Janet's team was working hard to close the month with good results. The previous month the team had missed its target on order entry by 2.45 percent in percentage of volume, and by 1 day, 6 hours in order aging. The current month had been about this miss; how it happened, why it happened, and action plans to correct it. Janet had meetings back to back where she had to explain, repeatedly, that this miss was not really a miss. Without adding any extra staff, since her group received 7.25 percent more orders than planned, the delay of only 2.45 percent past the fiscal month cutoff date was, in fact, overachievement.

Janet's manager, desperate to recognize revenue in the current month despite all other contributing factors, had turned, overnight, into a difficult, irrational, rather offensive leader, often humiliating her during meetings by calling out last month's performance a "disappointing miss," among other things. Her pushback about increased volume of orders had been labeled "a lame excuse," and Janet's stand in defending her team was being considered "indecisive leadership, aiming for failure."

This month Janet was determined to enter every single order in the system by cut-off date. The numbers looked promising, and,

> with a little push on the final stretch and minimal overtime, the team made it. Stepping with confidence into the meeting, Janet was shocked to find her manager livid and ranting because of her repeated poor performance. He was criticizing her performance on managing payroll hours, overtime spending, and, despite the fact that she had met her budget target for the month, her decision to have people come in on Saturday to finish entering the orders was being called "idiotic."

We have all seen this type of behavior. We've all lived through it, in one form or another. Many of us have this type of behavior to blame for one or more of our decisions to move on with our careers. Where is it coming from? This perfect recipe for disaster comes from a combination of factors: unbalanced, non-prioritized goals, swings in priorities from one extreme to the other, and knee-jerk, panicked reactions in leaders. This month—everyone runs like crazy to meet data entry goals. Next month—everyone runs like crazy to meet budget. The following month—we're the only business in the industry without a green program. Some leaders cannot understand—or do not value—the basic notions of stability, dependability, and consistency in laying out goals for their teams and managing performance. Others simply push things too far by setting unrealistic targets in complete ignorance of process capabilities, therefore generating unstable, fearful, demotivated environments, prone to internal conflict and high turnover.

On the flipside, sometimes leaders who drive this type of behaviors in their teams are not even aware of it. An intimidating, demanding leader must think before asking a simple question, because that simple question can have a downstream effect of panic and chaotic shifts in priorities.

When the company boat's edge is so close to the water, rocking that boat through rapid shifts in focus, or through erratic changes in direction, can be a bad idea. How can that be prevented, while implementing dramatic change, restructuring, and managing a complex turnaround plan? There are a number of measures, called the building blocks of performance:

Alignment with the Strategic Plan

In Chapter 4, we worked through defining an action plan, complete with key actions, owners, and a project manager to keep track of it all. That is the strategic plan for the turnaround effort. The more we adhere to it, the bigger our chances of survival, success, and delivery on—or ahead of—

schedule.

Two big temptations occur in such cases, both wasteful and hazardous:

- **Doubling back**—doubting the validity of the plan, after signing off on it, without new data and without a real cause for this doubt. Lingering in the muddy waters of "what if," rather than starting the plan's execution.
- **Finding "pet projects" to add on**—using EXPL's case study, let's assume Mr. Johnson, who was tasked with the outsourcing of the printing function, is asked, "You're already looking into this type of thing, can you also please explore some call-center outsourcing options?" One simple phrase and chaos has arrived. Now Johnson will be confused as to what would please his supervisor more; the fact that outsourcing printing is not on the project's critical path will create a false sense of security and he will, most likely, embark on a wild-goose chase, posing risk to the overall execution of the plan.

Both temptations are dangerous. Keeping everyone on task requires effort and decisive action. Keeping things simple can be like fighting a swarm of flies or—in sad, desperate cases—hornets.

Cross-Functional Visibility

In Chapter 4, we discussed the strategic plan. Let's identify Chris Jackson as the project manager for EXPL's turnaround plan execution. He is responsible for ensuring cross-functional visibility. The wire he's walking is a tough one, a fine balance between anti-silo initiatives and keeping everyone minding their own business. With complex plans, the key is to graph downstream impact flowcharts for all business units and work with clear visibility from there.

For example, everything that is changing in retail will impact customer service—therefore visibility is needed. There are few changes in the customer service process that will impact retail—therefore, visibility is optional, for information purposes only. If EXPL is reducing its inventory of vehicles, this has nothing to do with Human Resources—no visibility is needed there. Establishing key stakeholder lists for each action plan area, in addition to cross-functional visibility mechanisms will make sure nothing is overlooked.

Measuring Success (MARS: Metrics, Audience, Reporting, Schedule)

How do we measure success along the way? How can we even recognize it?

Establishing key performance indicators (KPIs) that make sense under the circumstances and are aligned with the strategic plan and its tasks, will ensure alignment and focus.

KPIs are, in this case, two types: goal measurement and stability control measurement. For example, if our goal is to reduce overhead costs in the head office operations by 60 percent, then the goal measurement is, obviously, the overhead spending in the head office—a dollar metric. Even if we reach that goal though, we can never be sure we didn't shoot ourselves in the foot from other angles, unless we establish a stability control metric to go along with it.

An example of such a metric can be customer satisfaction: surveyed and base-lined before the changes start, watched carefully after the changes begin: are we making our customers pay for our restructuring? Is the relationship with our customers in danger, and why?

More on how to get customer data, and how to get it to work for you, will be covered in Chapter 12.

Another example could be from the sales realm. A conversion rate would do the trick. We cannot use net sales or sales volume while the plan contains all kinds of close-out sales events and inventory liquidation actions. The potential bad signal could go unnoticed under the higher sales volume driven by these events. A rate would do, though—carefully chosen to be as little as possible—affected positively by other actions, so the output signal remains clear and visible.

Success documented, recognized, and celebrated without any shadow of a doubt, needs to come from MARS—metrics, audience, reporting, and schedule. We've talked about metrics. The audience represents the people who need to stay informed of the performance on the respective metrics—key stakeholders, all employees, investors, etc. Reporting speaks to the actual measurements or report generation. It's about how we measure, and how we distribute, document, and archive the results, together with the execution of the actual measurement process. The reporting team is also responsible for watching carefully the performance of KPIs versus set target levels, and for informing the key stakeholders immediately when one or more KPIs are underperforming. Raising the red flag is part of the job. Finally, the schedule of reporting and communication speaks to the frequency of reporting and distribution of measured data to the intended audiences. Some KPIs would be measured and reported daily, other KPIs would be measured weekly, monthly, or as needed.

Operating Mechanisms

How do we actually operate this plan? How do we meet, what we discuss, etc? The answer is we meet as little as possible, we discuss minimally—outside of decision-making processes. We work. We drive our teams and support our teams to deliver on the plan, to achieve the goals, to stay on task, and, let's not forget, stay with the company.

Some companies have a culture for a lot of meetings, under the generic umbrella "meeting is what leadership does." With the exception of strategic meetings, there could be better use of leadership time and resources: leadership should—yeah—lead! By example, by setting goals, targets, and challenges, by supporting the teams, making sure they have everything they need to be successful, by coaching, motivating, and retaining. By talking to the employees openly about their fears regarding their future, by explaining decisions so they can drive alignment and cohesion. By making sure office politics, disrespectful behaviors, and nonproductive attitudes never find a home in the business units. By making sure an employee looking for direction will always know where to find his or her leader, day and night. By working interference for them, removing roadblocks in their paths, and mediating their conflicts. By encouraging and rewarding bold action, enthusiasm, and courage.

This translates to only a few meetings, replaced by productive time in the office and swift, five-minute interactions as needed. The only meetings that should be making the cut in a turnaround are staff meetings—one with your team and one with your leaders and peers—once a week, and tollgate (milestone) reviews. Turnaround strategy meetings also need to happen in the initial phase. The rest should be set up only as needed, after serious pushback, and verification that:

- there is an agenda.
- the topics cannot be discussed during a five-minute visit, a conference call, or by email,

- everyone invited is actually needed, and
- no one needed is forgotten.

The excessive meeting trap is dangerous, hard to fight back, and, especially in financially troubled times, attractive. Who doesn't want to look busy and important when layoffs are scheduled for next month? Being in back-to-back meetings speaks to our personal insecurities. It calms our nerves and keeps us from thinking of our biggest fears. Scratch that . . . Keeps us from thinking, period.

Tollgate (Milestone) Reviews

These are important review meetings about the progress of the turnaround plan. This is where leadership meets and reviews actions taken and their success. If the actions taken were according to plan, are the results matching the forecast? If the in-house printing operation was outsourced, did it free up the cash flow as expected?

The tollgate reviews is the forum where the turnaround project team comes together and analyzes the results of (a part of) the execution: roadblocks, solutions, unplanned consequences—good and bad, added need for support and resources, revised commitments, and so on. This is the forum where the project team reviews the problem areas on the project dashboard.

There is a caveat here, and also for most meetings: there shouldn't be much effort put into beautifying the results and presenting them in a 30-page PowerPoint that could win an award for visual appeal. The project teams should focus on doing the task work, not on presenting the work. If a leader can't figure out the results of a project from Excel, a project file, or Word document, and absolutely needs a PowerPoint, formatted in a particular way—well, that is wasteful. This rule should stand for every working session or project milestone review. The exceptions to this rule are board presentations, bank / investor presentations, and anything for public review.

Aggressive Bonus Program

Money is the biggest motivator, especially for the employee of the company in financial distress, where "career" and "advancement" simply won't do it anymore. For a reward program to work, the incentive has to come immediately, be substantial enough to trigger changes in behavior, and be tied undisputedly into performance metrics that are established clearly. Ideally, this bonus would pay monthly, and, for the top performer, doubling or even tripling her annual income should become a possibility—it needs to be that aggressive.

Driving high performance is an important piece of the recovery plan, explained in detail in Chapter 27.

Chapter 7
Internal Strategic Alliances

Before hitting the gas pedal, the operations turnaround team has to secure firm commitment of support from a few critical functional departmental areas: Finance, Human Resources, Legal, and Information Technology. These functional areas have to be on board with the turnaround action plan; they have to establish operating mechanisms that will ensure proper and timely support of changes and actions taken by the turnaround project team. They have to define with accuracy the givens, lead times to implement changes, paperwork requirements, and any process needed to be in place, to ensure flawless execution with minimal cost and risk.

Finance

These employees will be able to assist in defining the key financial metrics and measures of success in a complex operational turnaround. They will be keeping their eyes on these metrics and, working hand in hand with the turnaround team, will advise of expected or unexpected results. Success cannot be claimed in any significant operational transformation without the financial confirmation of achieving the intended target.

Human Resources

HR is a critical partnership for any turnaround or restructuring action. These coworkers help implement the vision and execute the restructuring, while making sure everyone gets fair treatment, decent benefits, reasonable severance, and transition support. They are the employee advocates, but also the employer advocates. They ensure proper balance among priorities and can usually maintain a cool head in the entire heat of the action.

There are a few caveats with respect to this relationship:

- HR has to understand and embrace the reality that it is a support function, not a part of the decision-making team. The employees do not run operational departments or lead turnaround teams; they support the implementation of the turnaround team's action plan.
- Sometimes, on some occasions, HR will tend to be somewhat hungry for power; the workers will push to be involved in any decision, claiming risk avoidance and policy compliance as concerns. This opens the door to one of the most energy-draining processes ever encountered: group-manage. A close relative of group-think, group-manage will ensure no one ends up having any
- accountability for anything, no one speaks their mind in a loud, clear, and fact-based voice, everyone will avoid conflict even if it would be beneficial, and, yes, in such groups there are usually one—if not two—HR managers present. Sometimes the group-manage culture is encouraged by HR under the claim that "Deciding who will be best suited for the job should be a cross-functional effort." Here's another example, "This decision could impact multiple facets of the organization, so we all need to be involved in this process." How about, "Onboarding the new leader is not something we can leave to chance—let's get together and decide how best to plan this." What could these all end up having in common? Group-manage. Despite all of HR's good intentions, group-manage promotes mediocrity and strips the functional leaders of their ability to make quick, crisp decisions, and to apply them without delay. There's also a learning piece that is lost in group-manage; if the leader is empowered to decide on his own, the decisions will be tested in the real world immediately and the results will provide key learning for the leader: what worked, what didn't, approaches, methods, and so on. Therefore, faced with the next opportunity, the leader will have learned from his mistakes/successes and will have become a better leader. Group-manage strips all that learning opportunity away. What about, "Deciding who will be best suited for the job should be a cross-functional effort"? Is this a valid argument? Not in the least. Decision to hire should

belong to the leader responsible for the respective functional area. If A thinks B is the best person to help A reach his goals, then B should be the one hired or selected for the job. There shouldn't be any group-manage decision making around it. HR has different goals than Mr. A (hiring manager), so does every other cross-functional area that B—the candidate—will look at interacting with. Because there is no direct alignment in goals, there cannot be much effectiveness in the group-managed decision to hire Mr. or Ms. B. Management by committee or consensus is not suitable for all organizations, environments, or situations. However, the leader should consult his resources before deciding, thus making a more informed, fact-based decision.

- HR has to be able to respond quickly and effectively to the turnaround leader's requests, which sound somewhat like this, "Here's what we're going to do, please help me make it happen." HR is welcome to inspect the basis of the decision, to poke holes in it, or to educate the leader on possible pitfalls, but ultimately HR has to help implement the turnaround plan.

Legal

Especially when a significant amount of change is required, collaborating with Legal becomes important in keeping the company out of court. "Playing it safe" is the best way, especially in cash-shortage times, when a lawsuit can be the tipping point of a company's fate. Unfortunately, especially when cash is short and people tend to panic, the most careless, risky, "Let's wing this one" type of decision tends to happen, in a desperate attempt to secure immediate benefits from these actions. Cool heads are highly valued in these times, leaders who can hold their ground in times of pressure and still implement change safely. Legal is a key partner in such times, advising on risk and helping make things happen in a safe way.

Information Technology

Everything we touch these days impacts a system, a piece of hardware, or software, requires communication technology support or configuration changes. The IT group is a great partner to have, as it can make things happen in a more efficient way by providing the right technology in support of the change. With IT, it is best to have clear requirements as to what is needed and by when. IT can take things a bit too far sometimes, as they are mainly technology-loving people with a heart for upgrading and improving to the latest and greatest of systems and hardware. Which is great, but during a turnaround, they need to keep things to a minimum, from both time and cash perspectives. Ideally, the turnaround leader should establish a process to inform IT of all changes and obtain a dedicated resource to become a part of the team, watching for possible systems implications of actions taken. IT can establish priorities and develop a sense of urgency, reflected in adjusted times to execute, simplified implementation plans, adaptable methodologies, and flexible scoping.

Forging these strategic alliances within the organization ensures a great start for the operational turnaround effort, because it allows the partnering functional leaders the time and notice to free-up and reallocate resources, while maintaining business continuity. Establishing liaisons among departments for the duration of the turnaround project will ensure proper channels of communication are open all ways, and that the intended process is followed for resource selection and allocation, workload management, and time management against a strict calendar of deliverables.

Chapter 8
Voice of Employees

Your turnaround consultant will start the initial diagnosis by finding the root causes of failure, with a 360-degree view of the entire operation: people, process, and culture. Here's why: even if the turnaround action plan eliminates losses and the main causes of waste, failing to identify and fix the root causes that led to failure in the first place will result in a highly unstable turnaround action: an environment that will start falling apart seconds after you'd say all work is complete. A well-oiled turnaround action plan addresses these issues, together with the restructuring; thus, the result will be a stable operation, positioned for growth, flexible, and variable, complete with processes, policies, and culture to match.

Identifying the root causes of failure is a daunting task, as these causes might be deeply hidden in years of doing business a particular way, in layers and layers of paperwork, required forms, established mechanisms, and culture. However, there is a way to find that out: listen carefully to the voice of the employees. Your turnaround consultant is not an employee, and will be able to establish an atmosphere of confidentiality and security where employees will share their thoughts freely, without fear of reprisal.

Carefully chosen open-ended questions will lead the employees into sharing what they have noticed as problematic. These interviews will be held at all levels, from all departments, all ages, and all tenure groups. Younger employees notice obsolete policies and systems more accurately than older employees do. More tenured employees have a higher resistance to change, while newly hired employees have a more critical view of the business. More tenured employees have memories of how and what was being done when the company was profitable.

While collecting all this information from employees, the consultant carefully categorizes the feedback, establishing with additional questions how significant each issue is perceived to be, which area it is coming from—people, process, policy, or culture—and the timeline when the negative change appeared. The timeline is important because, through data analysis, it can reveal the corresponding change that took place and started generating problems: new leader, new system, new location, etc. Collecting VOE (voice of employees) in an organized manner is saving a lot of time and work. The worksheet shown in Fig. 8.1, a matrixed approach at collecting VOE, is enabling the interviewer to organize and categorize the data while collecting it. This aspect is valuable, due to the fact that the employee remains available for further clarifications, during the categorizing of their feedback. Additional columns can be inserted as needed, as it might be useful to capture other details, such as employee contact info, date of hire, etc.

Name	Unit	Level			Issue	Type				Impact			Timeline	Comments
Full name	Business Unit	Functional	Mid-Management	Executive	Description	People	Process	Policy	Culture	High	Med	Low	Date of noticed change	Additional info

Fig. 8.1. Table header for capturing voice of employees data.

Using a few examples, let's explore the matrixed approach to collecting and analyzing VOE.

Case Study 1

Interviewer: "Thank you for joining me today, I appreciate the opportunity to chat with you. I will start by saying that everything discussed here is entirely confidential, it will in no way be associated with your name or reported to your manager."
Employee 1: "Oh, ok, sure."
Interviewer: "I'm interested in learning what you see as not working properly in your area, what is causing you the most grief at work?"

Employee 1: "Well, I personally struggle with the attendance policy. I am not being lazy or disrespectful or planning to play hooky all day. I am trying to be a good employee, but I am also a single mom and my small children do get sick. And if I have to call in sick, I lose vacation time, but I also get a disciplinary action if someone else has booked that day off and there's no swap available."
Interviewer: "No swap available? What do you mean?"
Employee 1: "Our policy states clearly that there are only so many available spots for days off on any given day, to ensure production at capacity. Some days you have to fight for, or reserve a year in advance—like any day in December, for example. Other days, no one wants vacation on those days—Tuesdays in November are not high in demand. Those spots are dictated by how many swap employees are available—someone who can step in and do your job while you're gone. But when your kid gets sick, and daycare won't accept sick kids, you're in a jam; you have no option but to stay home with your kid, swap or no swap."
Interviewer: "So, if you call in sick on such a day, what happens?"
Employee 1: "I still get paid if I have available vacation accrued, but I also get a disciplinary action: step one, then two, then three, then fired. It doesn't really matter how good an employee I really am. Because of this, I am always in one or other step of disciplinary—they fall off my record, one by one, after six months of perfect attendance. Since I am always in disciplinary, I am never considered for promotions or raises, and I have never had a vacation since this whole thing started."
Interviewer: "When was that?"
Employee 1: "Some four years ago, in 2005, early spring. I was on maternity leave when they changed policies. Moreover, this year, due to financial problems, they reduced our paid time off by four days a year. It's even worse."
Interviewer: "Are you comfortable giving me your name and title? Department, maybe? Do you have an extension where I could call if I need more details?"
Employee 1: "Sure, my name is Linda Smith; I work in Returns, Receiving, 6118."

Based on this interview, the interviewer can fill in the first line of the VOE matrix, marking with an "x" the appropriate column(s) for level, type of failure, and impact.

Name	Unit	Level			Issue	Type				Impact			Timeline	Comments
Full name	Business Unit	Functional	Mid-Management	Executive	Description	People	Process	Policy	Culture	High	Med	Low	Date of noticed change	Additional info
Linda Smith	Receiving	x			Attendance policy issues for single parents, fast track to disciplinary and term			x		x			2005 Q1	Demotivated, discouraged, retention risk

Fig. 8.2. VOE data table, showing case study 1.

Case Study 2

Interviewer: “What do you see as problematic in your area, what is causing you the most grief at work?”

Employee 2: “Constant change. Nonstop change. Every day there is a different priority. I can’t live like this, work like this. Most of us here in IT cannot understand the benefits of half the changes we make, yet we are all educated individuals. There doesn’t seem to be a whole lot of strategy or vision, based on the zigzagging we’re constantly doing.”

Interviewer: “Could you please be more specific—maybe give me some examples?”

Employee 2: “Sure. Just a few months ago, a decision was made to change our existing reporting system and revise everything: collected data, queries, frequency, and storage of reports. We had barely got used to the new system when it was revised again, for no apparent reason, and reversed halfway to what it used to be. Guess what we’re supposed to be doing next week? A third revision of the same data reporting system. It’s disarming, discouraging, and it’s never over. The volume of work is huge, and every time we do such a revision we end up falling behind on our day-by-day tasks, so we have to put in overtime to get caught up.”

Interviewer: “Excellent example, thank you. You said you are in IT? What do you do?”

Employee 2: “I am a senior analyst.”

It's time to insert the second interview in the VOE matrix. What's different this time is that there are two lines needed, generated from the same interview, to capture the two failure modes the employee is describing: one has to do with change management, the other with goals and vision alignment.

Name	Unit	Level			Issue	Type				Impact			Timeline	Comments
Full name	Business Unit	Functional	Mid-Management	Executive	Description	People	Process	Policy	Culture	High	Med	Low	Date of noticed change	Additional info
Linda Smith	Receiving	x			Attendance policy issues for single parents, fast track to disciplinary and term			x		x			2005 Q1	Demotivated, discouraged, retention risk
Pete Jones	IT		x		Lack of change management		x			x			2008 Q4	Confused, frustrated, demotivated
Pete Jones	IT		x		Lack of alignment with company vision and goals		x			x			2005 Q3	Demotivated, lack of sense of direction

Fig. 8.3. VOE data table, showing case studies 1 and 2. Case study 2 generated a double entry.

Continuing on the path of VOE capture and categorizing, through interviews with open-ended questions, our VOE matrix can start looking like this:

Name	Unit	Level			Issue	Type				Impact			Timeline	Comments
Full name	Business Unit	Functional	Mid-Management	Executive	Description	People	Process	Policy	Culture	High	Med	Low	Date of noticed change	Additional info
Linda Smith	Receiving	x			Attendance policy issues for single parents, fast track to disciplinary and term			x		x			2005 Q1	Demotivated, discouraged, retention risk
Pete Jones	IT		x		Lack of change management		x			x			2008 Q4	Confused, frustrated, demotivated
Pete Jones	IT		x		Lack of alignment with company vision and goals		x			x			2005 Q3	Demotivated, lack of sense of direction
Alan Abrams	CS			x	Not encouraged to stand up for himself				x		x		2006 Q1	Bothered by lack of accountability and by lack of support from leaders
Abby McIntire	Sales Rep	x			People lacking selling skills bring dealership performance down	x	x			x			unsure - new hire	Ambitious yet demotivated by group performance metrics
Sheila Watson	Shipping		x		Continued pressure to cut costs, year after year	x	x		x				2005 Q2	Frustrated, demotivated. feels she's tasked with unreasonable demands
Adam Jones	Sourcing		x		Time spent traveling is not considered for overtime		x	x				x	2005 Q 2	Discouraged, tired, high retention risk

Fig. 8.4. Completed VOE data table.

In some cases, we have marked two types of failures to capture the failure mode; it can happen that both people and process participate in a failure mode.

Collecting the voice of employees was the first part of this process. The second part is analyzing all the data and drawing fact-based conclusions from it, followed by improvement initiatives that integrate in the turnaround plan.

Through a series of data manipulation and analytics, the data shows a cluster of points of origin around 2005 Q1–Q3, in our example. This cluster indicates the need to investigate and identify major changes that occurred about that time. Since hindsight is 20-20, with the help of this cluster, we might be able to identify what caused multiple failures, correct it, and take key learning from it.

Some common themes are also starting to show. One such common themes is demotivated employees, retention risk, and confusion. Process is the leading type of failure, followed by all the others, in a tie. Process failures are reported equally across the board, regardless of tenure or rank.

Based on these findings, the turnaround consultant can embed much-needed improvement in the turnaround action plan, thus securing a path to stabilization and a better, more productive environment. The common mistake in all troubled companies is to blame any and all dysfunctions on the financial state of the business, and to assume that it will all go away once we come out of the tunnel. Sometimes these dysfunctions are at the core of why the company is in need of a turnaround to begin with. Companies are made of people, and people cannot perform in a demotivating, confusing environment, and yield 100 percent creativity, dedication, and performance.

In some cases, with the use of new inexpensive technologies, it is relatively easy to set up and capture data from all employees. Once the categorizing exercise described above is completed, an anonymous survey can be created with questions probing specific areas. A carefully crafted survey will open with questions regarding the main dissatisfiers identified during the initial interviews. Then it can continue with open-ended questions, around what employees see as the greatest problems: product, policy, process, leadership, etc.

Case Study

An example could be as follows:
Please identify the top three issues you see as responsible for our company's current financial situation:

1. Product
    - Quality
    - Diversification
    - Customer perception and expectations
    - Pricing (too high or too low)
2. Service, maintenance, and repairs
    - Parts availability
    - Pricing (too high or too low)
3. Customer service
    - Quality
    - Hours of operations

- Customer service is not a companywide culture

4. Dealership sales
   - Commission structure
   - Local advertising
   - Trade-in program
   - Lease renewal
5. Advertising and promotions
   - Not effective or competitive
   - Irrelevant
   - Wrong channels (car ad in animal-themed magazine)
6. Customer policies
   - Not customer centric
   - Outdated
   - Nickel and diming the customer
   - Inflexible, unfriendly
7. Employee policies
   - Not employee centric
   - Outdated
   - Inflexible, unfriendly
   - Punitive
8. Company culture
   - Corporate communication
   - Career path, development
   - Achievable, relevant goals
   - Rewards and recognition
   - Pay levels
   - Benefits
   - Work/life balance
   - Fairness and consistency in employee treatment
9. Leadership
   - Trust and reliability, accessibility
   - Fairness
   - Change and change management
   - Unreasonable expectations
   - Long term focus, vision, strategy

This entire list of options can be repeated under the heading of "issues regarding employee satisfaction with current employment," or engagement, for example.

Most survey platforms come with analytics packages to help the consultant prioritize areas of focus by analyzing the frequency of particular themes. If one topic, for example, the attendance policy, only turns out to be an issue for 3 percent of the employees, then other, more often encountered, issues that turn out in larger percentages need to be addressed with higher priority. Voice of employees (VOE) is a powerful tool, if used and analyzed properly. There is a catch though: having the employees share what their thoughts are, and then failing to follow with action is a costly mistake, as the employees will become further disappointed and less willing to share their observations.

Any VOE exercise should be followed-up by promptly communicating to the employees that:

- their help was appreciated,
- their inputs have been noted,
- there will be actions developed from these inputs, and
- there will be further communication, both ways.

Once the VOE-based changes have been implemented, a good way to capitalize on these changes and increase employee morale and engagement is to ask for feedback from the employees about the effectiveness of the changes. Is the new attendance policy better? Do single parents of small children now have access to promotions and raises? Have we fixed the issue? It can be challenging, because no matter how good an employee can be, most business processes require their physical presence during their allocated shifts, and, in manufacturing, for instance, the absence of an employee can decrease production for an entire assembly line. However, such environments can come up with creative approaches to improve the employees' environment and work conditions.

VOE should not be a limited to a crisis exercise; it pays greatly to have a continuously open channel of communication with the employees, ensuring confidentiality and prompt response. Whether it is in the form of a survey, an "Ask Us" box, or Intranet online form, the channels should stay open and allow for rapid correction of concerns, as soon as they become issues.

Chapter 9
Recruiting the Players for the Turnaround Team

Who are the talented, dedicated members of the turnaround project team, and how do we find them? Your consultant will bring his or her team, but usually there is a need for more resources. Selecting the right people for this job is part of your consultant's job; a specific set of skills are required to be able to execute timely on a complex turnaround plan.

These resources should be selected from the human resources pool already on staff; no additional hiring required, with rare exceptions. The abilities required might vary to some extent, case by case, but they are largely around these lines:

- ✓ **High Intelligence Quotient**

Having significant brainpower is the key to success for any turnaround team player. A good mental capacity will help the team member handle conflicting priorities, complex situations, and multitasking, while keeping on track and deciding swiftly and correctly under pressure. An astute individual will be able to grasp business concepts and implications of actions faster and more accurately than the average employee will. A high degree of emotional intelligence is required, so that the player will mediate conflicts, negotiate through conflicts and disputes, read between the lines, and predict problems before they manifest. The high IQ is a prerequisite for versatility, in high demand for any such resource.

✓ Excellent Communication Skills

The ideal resource has the ability to communicate concisely, when needed, on task, through all channels and all means of communication, and can steer the team toward fast, to-the-point communication that works both ways. This person should be someone who is ready to verify that his or her message gets across properly, is not reluctant to explain further, can foresee and eliminate misunderstandings, be present to senior leadership, and address any questions. He or she needs to fearlessly enter rooms full of worried people and answer all their questions truthfully, assertively, to the point, in a manner that will drive staff retention and commitment. This individual needs to be equally comfortable delivering good news and bad news across the board. This is not the place for empty phrases and tedious lectures; this is the place for an honest, empathic, inspirational communicator.

✓ Courageous, Positive Attitude

Being a positive individual, one who believes in what she is doing, one who is self-confident to the point where her drive and determination are not diminished by doubt, anguish, and fear, is important for the success in this role. As this individual stands to implement abrupt change and, often enough, quite unpopular measures of cost cutting, she needs to have the confidence needed to face the consequent storm. She needs to be able to draw her strength from the realization that she makes a difference, and a big one. She should have the ability to gently push back on the territoriality and hostility of others, and considerately persuade them to implement changes, without engaging in non-constructive conflict, and without carrying grudges.

She also needs a strong backbone, as the above-mentioned hostility and pushback could get rough at times; she cannot let herself be intimidated. She is an accountable individual, one who acknowledges quickly both ownership and opportunity and has a good grip on deliverables. She is the type of individual who is not afraid to publicly announce expected dates of delivery on project results and what those results will be. Finally, she cannot be the type of individual who will let stress and job security concerns diminish her performance; thoughts of abandoning ship do not blend well with intentions to drive positive change.

✓ Excellent Follow-Through

This is the type of assignment where you need to be able to rely on the team member to complete her piece of the assignment on time, within budget, in sync with the other players; while keeping you informed of all developments. This is not the type of activity where you settle for being unsure, at any given time, whether or not a task is progressing per plan. You need to know for sure; therefore, exceptional follow-through is critical for the successful turnaround team player.

With these essential skills in mind, how can we identify accurately and rapidly the best-suited candidates for the turnaround project team? Do we even have such people in our midst? We would know if we would have them, wouldn't we? Well, not necessarily. Some of the single parents we have systematically ignored due to a faulty attendance policy might qualify. Let's keep in mind the environment, consisting of people, process, policies, and culture, has been proven faulty; therefore, the assumption that it was also faulty in recognizing employee value is a fair one.

One option in selecting these candidates is during the voice of employee interviews described in Chapter 8. During the interviews, your turnaround consultant will recognize these skills and will be able to probe further in search for the core material needed for a successful turnaround team resource.

A second option is to ask HR for help—not in the usual way though. If not clearly specified, HR will be happy to recommend politically correct people, team players in a traditional way, with good (read as average) results, and no spark. They would be decent, reliable folks who were never involved in any conflicts, nor stood up too firmly for their beliefs. Oh, and they would also have impeccable attendance.

Nope, for the type of achiever we need, the profile is surprisingly different. We welcome the determined rebels, the ambitious, overachiever, hungry for recognition and advancement, and the folks who will come in late now and then, but always check their email from home in the evening. They are the ones who are always reachable, because they care.

A list of telltale signs, in addition to the skills listed above, will look somewhat like this:

- Their backgrounds reflect a somewhat lower average of tenure with one employer: two to four years maximum, yet showing rapid growth and career advancement. A sad consequence of our corporate culture: ignore the overachiever from within, and choose to let ourselves be awed only by new hired talent. The ignored, saddened performer will soon get the message and will be able to make a great career move at a new company. Next company—same story, but they advance their careers this way.
- They have a reputation to be focused strictly on results, and a history of reaching and repeatedly exceeding goals.
- They have a history of proposing improvement, driving change, constantly thinking of newer and better ways to do things.
- They might have mentions in their files of previous conflicts or arguments with peers, superiors, or reports about business issues. They are known as outspoken and not shy. They are respectful to others, yet have stood up to bullies despite what was called "their best interest." They are not water-cooler politicians.
- They can come from all levels in the organization: from customer service representative to vice president. The turnaround team needs resources of all levels.

Based on this list, HR will be able to point out a few overachieving "troublemakers" to staff the turnaround project team. It will be somewhat like herding cats, but this combination is the most likely to yield significant results fast. Based on the rules of randomness, the people selected will find, to some degree, a natural fit between their respective areas of interest and expertise, and the available open spots on the team. The rest will fall into place, now that most pieces of the puzzle have been identified.

Chapter 10

Corporate Culture Evaluation

In any turnaround opportunity there is almost 100 percent probability the corporate culture is also in dire need of fixing. Moreover, the deteriorated corporate culture might have triggered chain-reaction process failures—behavioral and decisional. These failures would be leading to the overall losses in productivity, focus, and efficiency. In many cases, the downturn starts with—or is led by—the corporate culture. In other cases, culture is an immediate victim of a downturn led by external factors to which the organization fails to respond quickly and swiftly enough.

In all cases, a successful turnaround cannot become a sustainable solution unless the culture is changed. Otherwise, there is a high risk that a culture suited for a money-losing, inefficient, demotivating, low-performance environment will fail to evolve to suit and support the post-turnaround environment, thus becoming one of the detractors from a stable recovery. In short, corporate culture does not fix itself.

What is corporate culture? It is the unique way a company does things: the values, the practices, the "how" behind the "what," the traditions and manners in which things are done. Altogether, these represent the soul of a company. Looking beyond the "it is what it is" common misconception about corporate culture, behind every cultural trait—good or bad—there is a driver, someone or something responsible for that particular cultural trait. Great news! This means we can evaluate and fix a company's culture just as easy as we would do with any operational process.

Evaluating corporate culture starts by identifying if the traditional signs of a bad culture are present—and what they are. Let's explore some of the root causes, implications, and fixes for a few common such signs of trouble:

Fear

Scenario: Employees are afraid—afraid to present in a meeting—hands shaking, trembling voices, hesitant to answer questions that require them to express their personal opinions and beliefs, or to draw instant conclusions in front of a group. They are afraid to speak up. When asked if they have comments or objections on a subject, policy, or decision, all present will look down and/or discreetly check what their colleagues are doing; brief, lowered-eyelid glances probing for their colleagues' silent point of view. After the meeting though—some will meet in the hallways and briefly discuss their honest point of view with a few trusted colleagues, and sometimes put together a quick contingency plan, meant to make things work for a little while longer, despite all pressures.

Root cause: Open conversations are not encouraged, objections are—officially or unofficially—prohibited, and people who ask uncomfortable questions are treated disrespectfully, or might even be faced with unwanted consequences from their leaders. Public humiliation is often present in this culture, where someone making a presentation is at risk of being publicly scolded for bringing a new approach, out-of-the-box thinking, or for making a mistake. One or more top leaders in this organization do not want contributors on their team—they want silent, obedient followers. If carefully explored from this perspective, it is likely the history will show cases of employees reprimanded or even terminated for expressing unorthodox points of view, or for pointing out leadership or decisional errors.

Implications: The main and most destructive implication is in the decision-making process. Employees will become hesitant in their decisions, and, tamed by fear, will start deciding based on the criteria of "What would please my manager," or "What would keep me out of trouble," rather than "What's good for the business." Trying to guess what the manager would like to hear is one of the most damaging and costly fear-driven behaviors. Errors will go unreported; unrealistic plans will be built based on impossible assumptions; processes will be altered to please Attila the Hun and his vision, regardless of how costly and inefficient such vision might be.

Case Study

Out in the rain, at the smokers' corner, two employees were sipping their steaming coffee behind the main manufacturing building of Metalcraft Wonders LLC. Tina, the tallest worker, glances quickly around and, taking advantage of the moment of privacy, opens the conversation she'd been dying to have. "So, how did it go at the planning meeting today?"

"I survived," said her colleague with a deep sigh, "but I also kept my mouth shut. The manager signed up to reduce the manufacturing cycle time for the table stands to fewer than nine minutes each." Long sigh, again, eyes rolling up to the gray sky.

"Which one—the large table stand?"

"Yup."

"You can't be serious. The lathe takes ten minutes just to shape it, how about handling, finishing . . . ?"

"I know. We're screwed."

"Why didn't you say something? Why didn't anyone say something?"

Tina asked.

"And risk having him tear me apart in there? I don't want to be the one who rains on his parade and gets fired for that. Don't you remember what happened to Jim last year at the planning meeting? At least this gives me the time to look for another job."

The fix: Identify the people responsible for fostering the culture of fear. Remove them from the organization—a turnaround is no time for hesitation, or for allowing Attila the Hun the time to change his DNA and become Mr. Reasonable Guy. Retrain people to trust the organization again—speak openly to the leaders. Positively reinforce the message that it's ok to think, decide, and act on what's best for the business. Treat mistakes with humor and drive learning from them. Apologize for past mistakes—there's no shame in acknowledging and apologizing for a mistake—even governments are doing it! Make recognition public, keep criticism private. The workforce will gladly help with this change; after all, no one likes coming to work every day, thinking this is the day of his or her termination. Ultimately, review and adjust all recent planning, and make sure that only realistic forecasts are reflected in the plan.

Caveat: There's a significant difference between dictatorial leadership and results-driven leadership. A results-driven leader will listen if a worker objects to planning on an unrealistic cycle time, will examine the objection carefully, and make sure that the goals are not exceeding process capabilities. He will explain his decisions and make sure employees understand limitations and company priorities. He will also make sure that employees are confident they can achieve their goals, by understanding and eliminating potential constraints, lack of training, or methodology.

Cover-Ups

Scenario: An error was made, sometime ago, of some consequence, implications, and visibility. An employee spotted and brought to light the respective error, by taking the issue to her supervisor. Two days later, there is no evidence of this report in terms of action plan to correct the error or to drive any learning from it. Two months later—same deal; any reference to the said error is quickly covered with an abrupt change of topic. The said error will never again surface in open forums. It will be mentioned sometimes in whispers in the hallways and in close proximity to the infamous water cooler. In some cases, the error is a large one, with significant cost attached—in the millions of dollars range—therefore the "need" for a cover-up is proportionally more acute.

Root cause: There is no admission of errors, which would enable efficient damage control. There is no learning driven from errors, no sharing of experiences, and no positive reinforcement for discovering errors. This behavior thrives in a climate of fear. Similar to a three-sided symbiotic relationship, fear and cover-ups feed off the corporate host, but also off one another, enabling the other to exist, and to further damage the host organism. In this environment of fear, cover-ups are generated at all levels by a combination of factors, all in relationship with negative, sometimes even traumatic experiences the employees have had; these experiences constantly shape behaviors, decision-making and thought processes, resulting in a twisted reality where the example phrases quoted below actually make sense:

- "We can never talk about this subject again."
- "You should pretend you didn't notice."
- "I have to think of a different reason I could use to justify the numbers; mentioning the real one will get me fired."
- "I can't tell my manager about it; she'll think I carry a grudge against so-and-so."

Implications: Even the greatest decision-making discipline, if based on wrong data, will not generate any valuable output. Let's assume, for example, that ABC Inc. shouldn't have upgraded its technology at the time it decided to, a decision which is bringing serious cash-flow consequences in present days. The failure to discuss openly this decision, why it was made, what the givens were, what the anticipated benefits were, and what would be the best course of action to minimize the consequences, will only add to the risk and losses. There is also a structural danger; if errors are "buried" at various levels in the organization, senior leadership can become oblivious to serious issues, therefore unable to respond to such issues before they have a dramatic impact: loss of revenue, cash-flow issues, loss of customer confidence, systems and data security, etc.

The fix: Back to the symbiotic relationship point, the first step is to address the culture of fear—as shown above. With that out of the way, implementing a rigor around analyzing the reasons behind the errors is quite straightforward. This author refers to it as "the anatomy of a failure," somewhat similar to the IT project post-mortem analysis, only applied to any operational area where a significant error occurred or a project failed. The anatomy of a failure is a process geared at uncovering where errors were made and why, what assumptions were wrong and why, and what actions need to be implemented immediately, to both recognize what worked and fix what didn't.

In the early days of medicine as a science, it became obvious that healing was possible only after anatomy was fully understood, through observation and autopsies; therefore, anatomy is at the basis of any medical training since Hippocrates based his teachings on it, four centuries before our Common Era. Similarly, in any business environment, one cannot hope to fix or prevent what one does not fully comprehend. Most of all, the anatomy of a failure is not about punishing anyone; it's about documenting findings—good and bad—and driving further improvement in processes.

Caveat: Just like with any other cultural changes, this one is difficult to implement from the perspective of transitioning the employees from fear to safety. It takes a lot of educating before such transitions can occur. Just like feeling afraid, feeling safe has to be based on experience; it's not just a memo someone puts out. It takes some time to get there, but the results are well worth the effort.

Retention Issues

Scenario: People are leaving. Finding "new and exciting opportunities," "moving out-of-state," or "opening a new business," whatever the reason, they are leaving at a more accelerated rate than they used to, above the market average. Before they go, some companies interview them, in search for the reasons they decided to leave; in few cases, though, is something actually done about it.

Root cause: People leave their leaders, not their company. Quite a known fact, yet limited. In our particular case, there is also the fear of bankruptcy, financial stability concerns, as the employer struggles to survive. A turnaround is a challenging time, adding change and stress to plates already full. Fear of layoffs is another huge driver behind employees looking for better jobs elsewhere. All true; however, it all goes back to the leaders: are they addressing these issues openly and honestly? Are they encouraging employees to bring forward their concerns? Are they keeping employees informed with all aspects of the business, to create engagement and ownership?

Implications: If the mind of the employee is on an online career site posting or on next month's mortgage payment, the results of his work are mediocre, lacking speed, spark, and soul. Some employees describe their last weeks with a company as "Going through the motions, because my mind was already made." A general state of disengagement will soon follow, causing further damage.

The fix: Open and honest communication. Although it sounds like a cliché, it is not if it's done right. It should be pushed to the extreme of encouraging the employees not to lie if they have interviews scheduled, openly discussing job postings, career concerns, the employment market, and so on. Coming to work one day just to find the doors closed, or a termination notice, can be a traumatic event; everyone fears it at a deep level. It ties directly with our primal instinct of survival as individuals. Discussing it openly will help with the fear and anxiety levels. Quite the opposite of some common misconceptions, an employee will hesitate to leave the manager who will allow them to talk openly about other jobs, interviews, and stability concerns. When presented with an offer, an employee will carefully weigh the unknown—the new job—versus the comfortable familiarity of the current position. Furthermore, if company data is openly discussed—sales revenue challenges, trends, and concerns, needs to cut costs, etc.—the employees will engage and start pulling together for the recovery of the business.

Therefore, the fix to the retention problem is maintaining employees comfortably engaged, caring about the survival of the business as if it were their own.

Following these major signs of a bad culture, there are a few less poignant ones. Despite the apparent lower caliber, these should also be addressed, as they are indicators of existing failures.

- **Systematic overtime**—indicator of workload planning issues, possibly lack of training, of clear direction, or of conflicting priorities. Driver of employee burnout, safety risks, attrition, errors, and increased costs.
- **Bad-mouthing the company**—is nothing else but employee frustration boiling over; should be carefully listened to, because it is the voice of the employees. Issues identified should be addressed and communicated clearly—as solved or being looked into—not hushed up into censored silence. Employees should be encouraged to bring their issues forward openly, rather than lobbying in the hallways. Bad-mouthing the company leads to a negative atmosphere and employee disengagement. With today's social media engagement and online tools, such as Glassdoor.com, organizations should be particularly quick in addressing systematic employee dissatisfaction. A bad online reputation in the labor marketplace can significantly hinder a company's ability to attract and retain good talent.
- **Long, back-to-back meetings**—sign of teams not able to reach agreements, make decisions, and align on issues in an expedited manner. The root causes should be examined and addressed; it could be an issue of poor alignment on goals and objectives, of conflicting priorities, or of a bad habit known as meeting addiction. Long meetings are driving employee burnout, and a sense of powerlessness and lack of control.
- **Absence of constructive conflict**—sign of fear-driven behaviors stumping the growth of revolutionary ideas and solutions. This leads to a mediocre, yet safe behavior, where doing what's usually done will be the outcome of every meeting.
- **Urgent non-emergencies**—sign of bad judgment, resulting in the allocation of top-tier resources to low priorities. An escalated

customer call belongs with the escalations department in customer service. It does not belong being transferred to the cell phone of a vice president, thus disrupting a strategy meeting. It does not constitute a real emergency, and it should not be treated as one. These urgent non-emergencies feed off the lack of understanding, or engaging, of the processes. For example, escalations are part of any customer service process and are no reason for panic. Such non-emergencies, upgraded without reason to an undeserved crisis status, are responsible for panicked behaviors and cover-ups; they represent a manifestation of "constant crisis" work mode.

After examining the signs of a bad culture, a look at the signs of a good culture is equally valuable. Just like with the bad, knowing what the good looks like will help identify and understand it. These are indicators of success in particular areas, allowing for further development of the good trends and using it as leverage against the bad trends.

- ✓ **Internal referrals for job openings**—sign that employees are happy with the company, willing to recommend it to family and friends. Helps create a strong, united workforce, helps tremendously with retention.
- ✓ **Good retention**—quite the obvious. Employees will remain with a company where they feel appreciated and rewarded.
- ✓ **Internal development and career paths**—a sign of recognizing value, encouraging individual development and offering growth and opportunity to the employees.
- ✓ **High engagement levels**—a good sign the employees give their best and care about what happens to the company. This is extremely important in the execution of successful turnarounds, as it helps employee alignment and rapid response to challenging priorities and deliverables.

Rather than searching for the perfect definition of ideal corporate culture and striving to achieve it, the simple way to define it is this: "A culture where people care about each other and their goals." This chapter does not aspire to be the theory of organizational culture; rather an analysis of what is in need of fixing from the pragmatic perspective, so that the turnaround action is stable and delivers, while fostering an environment which employees would call "their second family."

Chapter 11
No Taboos

In both the operational and the cultural aspects of the successful turnaround execution, there can be no taboos. The biggest benefit the turnaround consultant will bring to the table is the objectivity with respect to actions and recommendations. For turnaround consultants, there are no emotional ties to this or that aspect of the culture or the operation; they did not implement the project that will now be closed down. Nor did they participate in the founding of the new manufacturing wing, therefore they are not hesitant in shutting it down.

For the internal employee, no matter how determined they might be in executing the turnaround plan, there is a psychological barrier, visible or not, that will dictate the priority in which things will be done, or the actual selection of actions. For example—and this is a common example—the employee will allow in many cases his/her emotional attachment to people, processes, personal beliefs as to what is right or wrong, or preconceived notions, to become a decisive factor in the restructuring initiative. The example phrases listed below are an illustration of such thought processes. Whether they end up being voiced publicly or not, they might be sitting at the core of the decision-making process behind the turnaround plan:

- "We shouldn't be giving up the centralized processing of returns; we were thrilled back in the day when we first implemented it."
- "It's always been done like that—we can't change it."
- "We can't suggest restructuring in the Media department, that's the CEO's favorite."

- "Let's try to cut more from customer service than other departments; all the rest are more important, more strategic (and someone else is managing customer service, not me)."
- "No one will like it."
- "It's our tradition."
- "It's someone else's problem."
- "Let's outsource every department but mine."
- "How can I make sure my job, function, and span of control come out unblemished from the turnaround action?"
- "Is there an opportunity for me to increase my income or span of control? What should I be focusing on to get positioned better after the storm? What should be on the first page of my secret agenda?"

These example phrases were chosen to illustrate the psychological barrier brought by the emotional ties of internal employees with the company's culture and processes, including some personal interest or concern ballast. That is because usually the lines are blurred: what is a taboo and where does the individual's concern for his/her own well-being, career, and interests kick in? For the sake of an easier illustration and argument, let's consider them all to be taboos, because, at the end of the day, they equally influence and corrupt the decision-making process.

Going back to the external turnaround consultant alternative, there is considerable reason to be confident such concerns do not limit the thinking of the external expert. Objectivity and keenness are to be expected, based on his or her ability to assess every aspect of the business in a taboo-free state of mind, without emotion; therefore, a data-driven, decision-making discipline can be achieved.

However, the consultant can only recommend; these are the limitations of the job. A consultant cannot decide for the business; the decisions belong with the leadership and, therefore, understanding of the recommendations and the determination to implement—both have to happen from those in charge. Even if, for some recommendations, there will be significant push-back from the leaders, at least the conversation is taking place about the subject. How else can we make sure we've covered all bases and that all pushback is of the valid, objective kind?

Sometimes, getting the necessary buy-in from process owners and leaders can be a challenge; multiple types of objections will be raised, and not all of them will be legitimate or constructive. This is the time for all to be reminded that there is no time; decisiveness is key, and so are the speed and the quality of execution. Clear, open, two-way communication will help with these situations, and also with discerning which of the objections are driven by fear for one's own security, and which come from a taboo mind-frame. Addressing both types of objections with adequate tools and solutions will clear the way of all roadblocks, enabling the turnaround team to start immediate execution of the agreed-on plan.

More on such tools and how to use them will be covered in Chapter 25.

Chapter 12
Voice of Customer

Do we listen, understand, and care about our customers? Most organizations would answer without hesitation: "Yes!" However, that is not always the case. Whether is not done in a methodical, practical way, or it is used to create exception-based processes, there is a lot of room for improvement. Listed below are a few common misconceptions about how to best care for one's customers.

The Exception-Based Process

Let's say, for instance, that a customer has a secondary failure quite soon after having to purchase a replacement for a defective part—out of warranty. No surprise, this is a big dissatisfier for any customer. Therefore, the customer service department, in cooperation with other related departments, decides to treat such cases by allowing the service representative some leeway in determining whether the customer should be charged for the second part replacement. On a case-by-case basis, the service representative is also allowed to send the customer some form of gift, meant at compensating the customer for the unpleasant experience with the product. Although this might seem to be a customer-friendly process, in reality it is not. Let's examine the steps needed to turn this exception-based process into a customer-centric process:

- Standardize all service processes; regardless of who the customer will speak to, they should be getting the same handling.
- Analyze the data behind the repetitive failures and establish a standardized, customer-friendly process to ensure proper service is provided. For example, establish a "parts warranty" policy, to

ensure the replacement part is also covered for defects for X amount of time.

- Eliminate all gift-giving policies; they do not do any service to customers. They lead to “pseudo” service calls, in which some customers will try to get some free stuff without having a real issue.
- Track all customer issues that do not fall under any of the existing standard operating procedures (SOPs), categorize them, and build SOPs for them.
- Ensure proper SOP is being followed throughout the organization for any customer issue, thus ensuring the service provided is consistent, efficient, and high quality.
- Finally, on any touch point with the customers, capture their feedback. More on this in a bit.

The Escalation to the VP Level—Or Above

Using the previous example, let’s assume the secondary failure has aggravated the customer to the point where she does not wish to speak to a service representative anymore. The customer asks for—and receives—the name and number of the vice president of Customer Operations. The customer then calls the VP, who will storm out of a turnaround strategy meeting to take 45 minutes of customer complaints via his cell phone. The VP does this because this is what is demanded of him by the apparently customer-focused culture at our example company; he wants to care for the customers, but knows no other way.

At the end of the 45-minute conversation, the VP will probably end up approving an even greater gift card for the customer, plus free parts with free installation. He made one customer happy, spent much more money than what the initial margin had been on the respective product, and spent zero time on implementing or driving change for a systemic fix.

Let’s take this VP escalation example, drive some learning from it, and turn it into a customer-centric process:

- In any service organizations there will be escalations; build process for them by answering these questions:
    - What constitutes an escalation?
    - Who should handle it: team, size, qualifications, location, and hours of service.
    - How should we handle escalations?

    - How to transfer or refer customers to the escalations team.
    - How do we measure their performance? Establish metrics and targets for the escalations team.
- Launch the escalations team, based on the process designed above, staffed with trained and empowered employees.
- Data and analytics support driving knowledge from analyzing the reasons leading to escalations: What makes our customers mad? How can we improve?
- Clear, systemic guidelines for addressing the customer issues, focused on fixing the root cause for the customers' problems.
- On-going trends analysis for key metrics and continuous improvement initiatives.
- Systematic knowledge transfer to cross-functional areas based on root-cause findings, to drive further improvement of both product and service.
- Train the senior leadership into using the newly formed escalations team: no trumping them, no exceptions, and no calls taken at VP level, or at any level above the escalation team.

We Know What Our Customers Want

This statement belongs with organizations that systematically survey their customers and drive their knowledge from the data collected. In all other cases, it's nothing more than a misperception, based on some limited understanding of customer behaviors, and some aged knowledge from years ago, when we had some information come our way. Strangely enough, this phrase is at the core of many product and service diversification or modification decisions, made in the latter companies.

Here's an example: an e-commerce business, selling music CDs. Based on current trends, a decision is made to "go green" in terms of the packaging used to ship the products to the consumers. The main argument that was made in this decision-making process was, "We know what our customers want—everyone is interested in green now; green is hot." So the necessary changes in processes, suppliers, and machinery were made to get the company in position to advertise their newly gained "green" status. Did this costly change help with sales numbers? The company did not notice any significant increase in revenue. So, is green a factor in the purchasing decisions of our customers? Obviously, it's not. Then, what is?

Let's turn this into a customer-centric initiative to improve the product and service offering of our example online music store, by following these steps:

- Find out what the real deterrents to purchase are for our particular customers: build an online exit survey, to pop up after exiting the company's website if the exit happens without checking out (no purchase made).
- Make the survey brief—no one has time. Ask to-the-point, key questions: What kept you from purchasing? Include an open comments field to allow you to capture some knowledge about your customers
- Capture the responses and build a Pareto diagram of all the main deterrents to purchase. It could look like this:

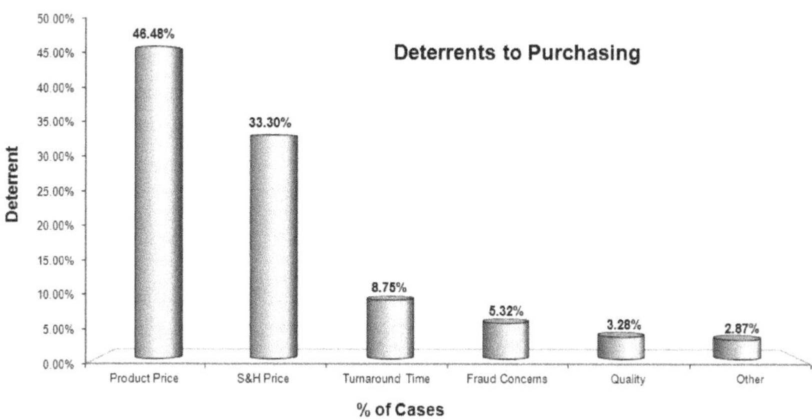

Fig. 12.1. Voice of customer (VOC) analysis of deterrents to purchasing.

- Build an action plan to address these deterrents and implement, while continuing to monitor new data.

By analyzing the Pareto diagram, we find that "green" didn't even make the chart; no wonder going green didn't make any difference in the customers' decision to buy.

There is an immediate, zero-cost fix we could apply: to address the fourth bar, "Fraud Concerns." All we should be doing is offer PayPal as an additional method of payment, therefore mitigating the concerns of some credit card users.

The first two bars are ultimately price-related concerns; whether the product is perceived as being too expensive, or our shipping and handling seems to be a bit too much, or both, together these two add up to 79.78 percent of the deterrents to purchase. Definitely worth investigating—we have found our biggest deterrent.

The third bar is also worth looking into—why is it taking us so long to ship and what are the consumer expectations? The modern consumers have their expectations educated by customer-centric environments, such as Netflix and Zappos (less than 48 hours to receive your order). Can we get there? How fast, how costly?

The fifth bar is represented by product quality concerns. Another example of further need to investigate: are we getting a bad quality reputation out there? What's the basis for these concerns? In this example, and any similar case, there is great value in benchmarking the data against the industry. Knowing what to shoot for is important for a customer-centric approach to balance cost cutting and growth.

The ecommerce example above is leading to the next topic: collecting and analyzing voice of customer (VOC) data.

For VOC data to be valuable and make a difference in a customer-centric turnaround, it needs to be precise, actionable, and recent. Therefore, deciding on the method of capture should be based on the reason driving the need.

Capturing the Voice of the Customer

Surveys

Most commonly encountered, surveys allow the capture and analysis of voice of customer data at various points of interaction with the business. A good survey tool has to be built based on the answers to the following questions:

- What are we trying to find out?
- Who is our target customer?
- Which is the best customer touch point to gather data?
- How do we motivate the customer to take time to respond?
- What constitutes a reasonable sample size for our survey?

Based on these answers, we will then be able to construct the wording of our survey questions, establish a frequency for data pulls (that is, weekly data pulls), create and document the methods to analyze the data—to ensure consistent analysis on each batch.

In some cases, we might be able to benchmark some of the data, therefore having some insight about where our performance sits within the industry. In other cases, where benchmarking is not an option, we establish a baseline; analyze and document current findings, with no rearview visibility—everything starts today. Then, on the significant measures identified, we start trends analysis as time passes, thus identifying what improvements we are driving in the perception of our customers.

Focus Groups

Focus groups are relaxed, casual conversations with a chosen topic, in a round-table type of environment. These will not generate large amounts of new data; they are used best to clarify perceptions or gain depth on the issues uncovered in surveys. For obvious reasons, focus groups are easier to set up for employees than for customers; however a focus group with customers can be the method of choice when looking to gauge the customer reaction to significant product changes or pilot programs.

Case Studies

Essential for the study and validation of our processes, products, and services, case studies allow insight into the performance of the same. Let's say, for example, we have a particular warranty service process and we'd like to assess if it is customer-focused, Does it address the needs of both the business and the customer? Is it up-to-par with the industry and the consumer expectations? Are we generating waste in this process? Are we generating consumer complaints? Are we losing sales due to an unfriendly process?

These questions can be answered by studying relevant cases involving warranty service. The cases we study can be real, from the archives of the business, or fictitious what-if scenarios. The data gathered from surveys can be analyzed comparatively and synced with the case studies. From here, driving improvement to the process is both customer-centric and watertight.

Existing Data Analysis

In any organization, there are significant amounts of data being collected. Extracting VOC data from the existing data should be an ongoing exercise, as it reveals important knowledge, with significant financial impact on the business.

An example of such VOC data extracted from existing data is, using the escalation example above, analyzing the reasons to escalate. An easy capture, every time a customer issue is escalated, a reason code can be attached. These reason codes can be analyzed and the main categories can be addressed with action plans. Improvement will be quantifiable. With key data such as this, on-going trends analysis should become part of the organization's dashboard. Keeping an eye on trends allows an immediate visibility and response on an issue that is reflected in the voice of the customer and the effect of changes being made in the operational sphere.

Net Promoter Score (NPS)

NPS (developed by Frederick F. Reichheld) has a lot of controversy around it, regarding its relevance and usefulness. NPS is a score calculated with a specific formula, based on the answers to the following question, "Based on your experience, how likely are you to recommend our product / service to friends or family?" The answers are captured on a scale from zero (0)—not at all likely, to 10—highly likely. The answers between 0 and 6 are considered detractors, 7 and 8 are passives, and 9–10 are promoters. Therefore,

NPS = percent promoters – percent detractors

NPS capture can be part of any customer survey, as it reflects overall how well we did at the respective touch point where the survey is being administered. NPS will be a skewed measure at the customer touch points that start from a bad experience. For example, within the same company, a survey for all new customers will generate a much higher NPS than the survey applied to customers calling in with out-of-warranty product defects.

Depending on the nature of the business, NPS is important to some businesses—obviously those where referrals are important drivers of new business. Tracking NPS is, consequently, the ultimate measure of customer satisfaction, reflected in new business generation.

Keeping Track of It All

How can we accurately keep track of all these metrics, plus the contexts in which the data was collected? Let us not forget any possible special cause, external factors. Oh, and we're also in the middle of a turnaround, therefore the amount of change we are driving is significant.

This author's recommended method to keep track of it all, XPeTrack (for Expedient Tracking), is a matrixed system that reflects in a visual manner the trends of key success indicators (service levels, customer satisfaction), synchronized with special cause events, project launch dates, campaigns—in short, anything of significant impact to customer satisfaction levels.

Methodology—XpeTrack

Using yet another example, we will start tracking the key metrics, projects, and events for an operational environment, in sync with key customer deliverable metrics and customer satisfaction score. During a period of 14 weeks, numbered 1 through 14, we will consider four special cause events with potential impact on one or more key metrics, and three projects/actions, also with potential impact on selected KPIs. These are:

1. Special cause incidents or events
   - Distribution center fire—week 7
   - Distribution center reopens after renovation—week 11
   - A TV show features our product during prime time—week 13
   - Nationwide syndication of the above TV show—week 14
2. Projects or actions
   - Online sales process improvement, implemented in week 3
   - TV ad campaign span, running weeks 1 through 8
   - Customer-centric warranty policy revision, implemented in week 5

   We will begin by adding one metric—service level in delivery, for example.

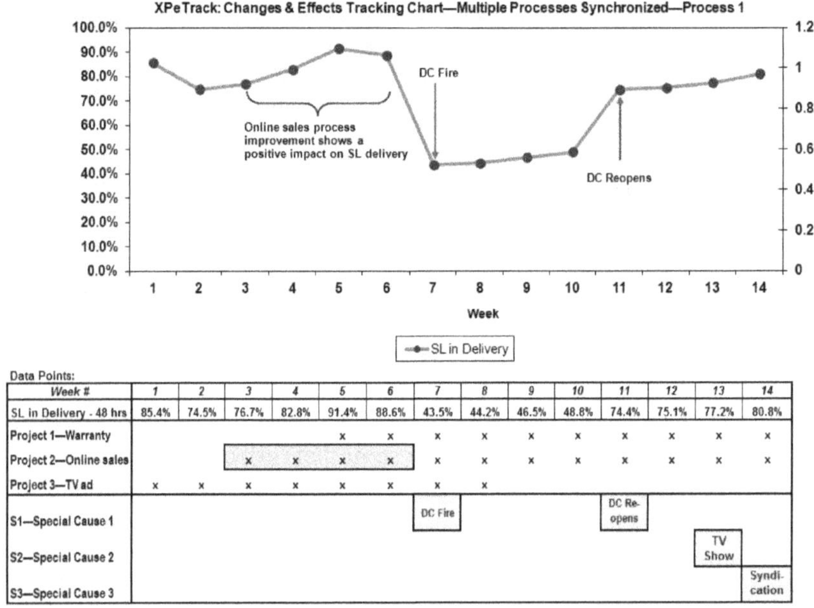

Week #	1	2	3	4	5	6	7	8	9	10	11	12	13	14
SL in Delivery - 48 hrs	85.4%	74.5%	76.7%	82.8%	91.4%	88.6%	43.5%	44.2%	46.5%	48.8%	74.4%	75.1%	77.2%	80.8%
Project 1—Warranty					x	x	x	x	x	x	x	x	x	x
Project 2—Online sales			x	x	x	x	x	x	x	x	x	x	x	x
Project 3—TV ad	x	x	x	x	x	x	x	x						
S1—Special Cause 1							DC Fire				DC Re-opens			
S2—Special Cause 2													TV Show	
S3—Special Cause 3														Syndi-cation

Fig. 12.2. XPeTrack: Changes and effects tracking chart—multiple processes synchronized—service level in delivery.

As it becomes immediately visible, in week 7, service level (SL) in delivery had a lot to suffer from a special cause event—the distribution center fire. SL in delivery recovered almost completely in week 11—when the DC reopened. This special cause and its effect are obvious and easy to catch.

Not so easy to catch is a trend impacted by a process improvement implementation. Weeks 3 to 6, we are able to see that the online sales process improvement had no adverse impact on service level in delivery—quite the opposite. We are also noticing that the TV show featuring the product on Channel 5 during prime time has no impact on delivery; nor does the syndication of the same show. It shouldn't have.

Let's continue by exploring a second key metric's performance in conjunction with these events, projects, and actions. This time we will chart sales lead conversion rate.

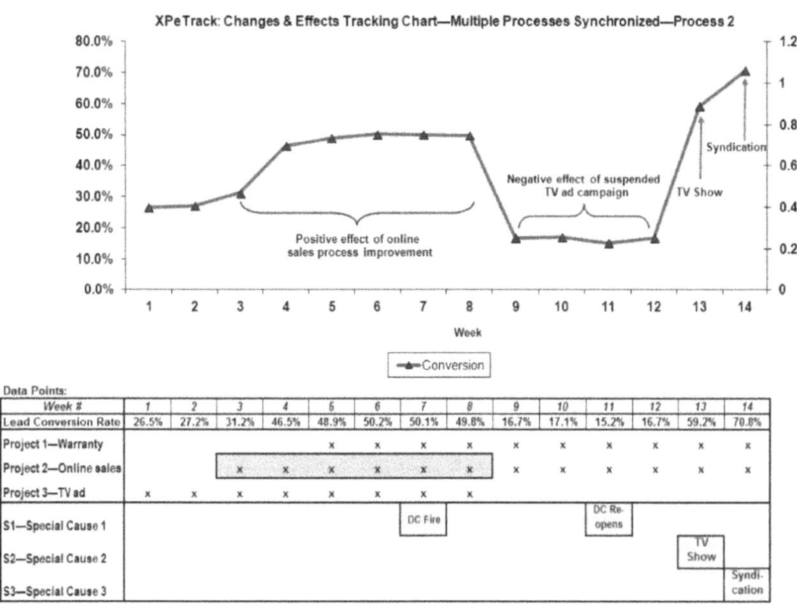

Week #	1	2	3	4	5	6	7	8	9	10	11	12	13	14
Lead Conversion Rate	26.5%	27.2%	31.2%	46.5%	48.9%	50.2%	50.1%	49.8%	16.7%	17.1%	15.2%	16.7%	59.2%	70.8%
Project 1—Warranty					x	x	x	x	x	x	x	x	x	x
Project 2—Online sales			x	x	x	x	x	x	x	x	x	x	x	x
Project 3—TV ad	x	x	x	x	x	x	x	x						
S1—Special Cause 1							DC Fire				DC Re-opens			
S2—Special Cause 2													TV Show	
S3—Special Cause 3														Syndi-cation

Fig. 12.3. XPeTrack: Changes and effects tracking chart—multiple processes synchronized—lead conversion rate.

In weeks 3 through 8, we are able to notice the positive effect of the online sales process improvement. The delta between the initial value (~ 26 percent), and the weeks 4–8 average rate (~49 percent), shows the net benefit of the online sales process improvement, because the rate of 26 percent prior to week 4 was a rate achieved while the TV ad campaign was running. The positive effect of the online sales process improvement is most likely continuing past week 8, but it is hidden by the negative impact of the suspended TV ad campaign. Once the TV show and the national syndication happen in weeks 13 and 14, the conversion rate hit unprecedented high values. The distribution center fire and, respectively, reopen have no visible effect on conversion rates—which makes sense.

For a third metric, we will choose customer satisfaction score (CSS). If measured and analyzed correctly, CSS offers direct visibility to our ability to satisfy customers with our products and services. Therefore, when assessing the impact of policy changes, campaigns, or business process reengineering, keeping an eye on customer satisfaction will validate if our actions are, indeed, customer centric.

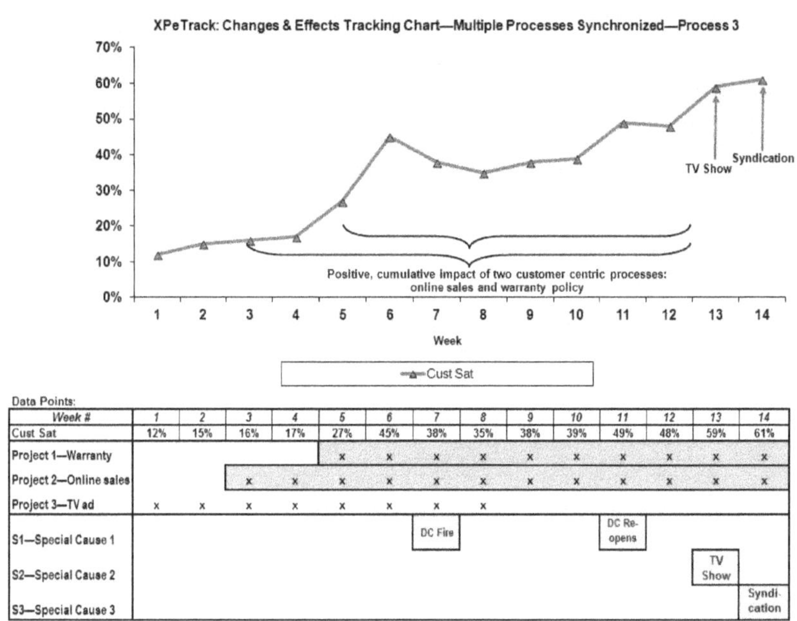

Data Points:

Week #	1	2	3	4	5	6	7	8	9	10	11	12	13	14
Cust Sat	12%	15%	16%	17%	27%	45%	38%	35%	38%	39%	49%	48%	59%	61%
Project 1—Warranty					x	x	x	x	x	x	x	x	x	x
Project 2—Online sales			x	x	x	x	x	x	x	x	x	x	x	x
Project 3—TV ad	x	x	x	x	x	x	x	x						
S1—Special Cause 1							DC Fire				DC Re-opens			
S2—Special Cause 2													TV Show	
S3—Special Cause 3														Syndi-cation

Fig. 12.4. XPeTrack: Changes and effects tracking chart—multiple processes synchronized—customer satisfaction score (CSS).

Charting customer satisfaction score will show the positive effect of the online sales process improvement starting to show on week 3, followed closely by yet another positive effect generated by the warranty policy revision. This CSS is definitely headed in the right direction. The TV show and its syndication in weeks 13 and 14 are reflecting a potential positive impact; to be sure we would need more data points to validate this growth is in direct correlation with these special cause events. Customers feel more positive about their experiences with a product or service if it is featured positively on TV, as it revalidates their decision to purchase. However, giving this set of data more time to mature will be able to give us the quantifiable benefit of such a TV feature.

These three key metrics we have charted—service level in delivery, lead conversion rate, and customer satisfaction score—can be shown together on the same chart (see Fig. 12.5).

Although it creates a busy look, and is not recommended to be loaded with more than 3–5 KPIs without analysis software support, the compounded view will allow a quick, rearview mirror look at the effect of special causes—marked with arrows. From the compounded view, we can work backward: if we notice common points of inflexion in our charts, or if we want to examine one or more KPIs performance in conjunction with others, and we are noticing common trends, this compounded view allows for the investigation into root causes to happen without delay, error, omission, or hesitation.

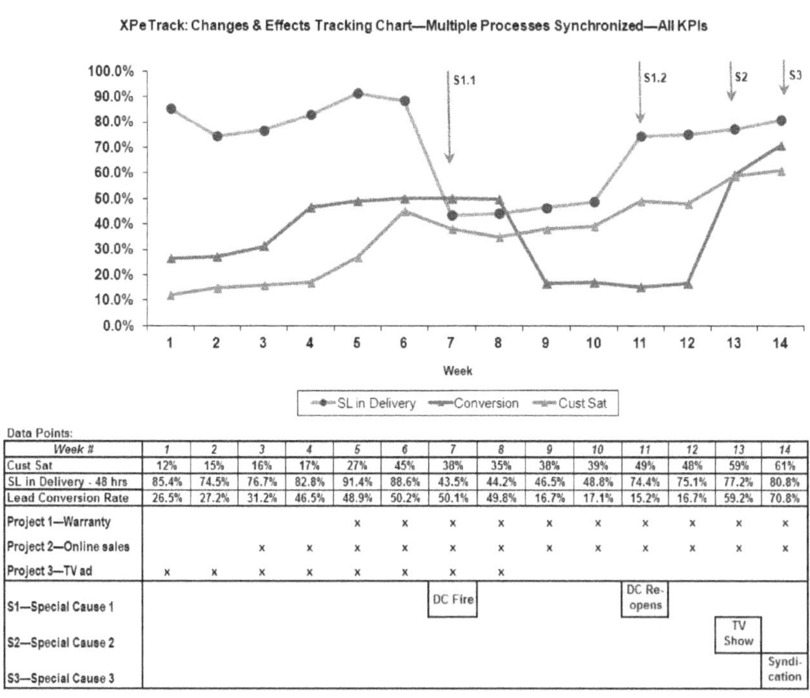

Data Points:

Week #	1	2	3	4	5	6	7	8	9	10	11	12	13	14
Cust Sat	12%	15%	16%	17%	27%	45%	38%	35%	38%	39%	49%	48%	59%	61%
SL in Delivery - 48 hrs	85.4%	74.5%	76.7%	82.8%	91.4%	88.6%	43.5%	44.2%	46.5%	48.8%	74.4%	75.1%	77.2%	80.8%
Lead Conversion Rate	26.5%	27.2%	31.2%	46.5%	48.9%	50.2%	50.1%	49.8%	16.7%	17.1%	15.2%	16.7%	59.2%	70.8%
Project 1—Warranty					x	x	x	x	x	x	x	x	x	x
Project 2—Online sales			x	x	x	x	x	x	x	x	x	x	x	x
Project 3—TV ad	x	x	x	x	x	x	x	x						
S1—Special Cause 1							DC Fire				DC Re-opens			
S2—Special Cause 2													TV Show	
S3—Special Cause 3														Syndi-cation

Fig. 12.5. XPeTrack: Changes and effects tracking chart—multiple processes synchronized—all KPIs.

Chapter 13
Who Is in Charge?

A turnaround is one of the most demanding times a company's employees could go through, including constant change, restructuring, uncertainty, resources spread thin, stress, panic, and confusion. In many cases, this state of chaos is something that has an easy fix: reintroducing the authoritative, formalized leadership model.

In North America, in recent decades, the collaborative leadership model has inserted itself, gradually replacing hierarchical models based on clear chains of command and authoritative stances. Together with business-casual dress codes and jeans Fridays, this model was meant to encourage individual engagement, ownership, and commitment, in an open, friendly environment, which fosters creativity and open communication, and rewards achievement regardless of role.

This model allows unlimited kudos messaging but restricts criticism, as it intends to provide a positive look and feel to every aspect. This model is responsible for the disappearance of reserved parking spots and corner offices. The intentions behind the collaborative leadership model are all good; this inspirational approach is based on the ability to get everyone motivated to do their best.

However, in real life this model requires enormous amounts of energy and leadership resources to be successful, and includes walking a fine line between corporate priorities and employee-driven policies. While these values can exist and yield successful results when sales numbers are on target and the business is making lots of money, they will quickly disappear when faced with financial hardship and insecurity. That is when a clear chain of command and authoritative leaders are needed.

For the duration of the operational turnaround planning and execution, a formalized, authoritative leadership structure must be put into place, announced, and enforced. Let's examine a few advantages brought by this change:

Focus on Results—The "What" Rather than the "How"

During turnarounds, the results are critical to survival; there is no time for "taking it easy," "breaking it gently," or "making sure everyone feels the same." Although the method might generate some amounts of blood on the highway, the need for speed and delivery supersedes everything else. Results must be achieved, measured, documented, recognized, and rewarded—promptly.

Ownership of Results

If the department leader approves all changes, he or she is solely responsible for the results. The collaborative leadership model allows for some pep rallying and beating around the bush, with the intention of creating consensus, unity around goals, and team spirit. A turnaround does not allow time for that. At each level, the leader, after analyzing the data, will make decisions. His direct reports will turn his decisions into actions, thus executing his vision. Objections are welcome; sometimes, they will change a decision, while other times they will be overruled. Whatever the outcome, the final plan will be executed immediately. Employees are welcome to ask for clarification about direction; the department leader will have to state clearly his expectations, as this will tie in directly with the precision and speed of the execution. It's all black-and-white . . . no gray area, dotted-line type of leadership.

Sometimes, in collaborative leadership environments, when times get rough, as they begin feeling threatened, some leaders will impose unrealistic goals and refuse dialogue with their employees, pushing them to "make it happen." This corporate version of "have my cake and eat it too" is responsible for preventing constructive dialogue from taking place between leader and employee. Such dialogue should focus on the strategy for the operational unit and the limitations of the process. Instead, it becomes a back-and-forth around getting the leader to accept the process capabilities and discuss priorities, or on getting the employee to sign up for the unrealistic goal and deliver it. This originates from the lack of ownership of results at the leader's level, and also from the leader's inability to understand the limitations and come up with a plan that makes sense.

Increased Speed and Accountability in Decision Making

The decision-making process is stripped of all circumstantial cross-functional involvement. Every department head is focused on his or her deliverables and informs the cross-functional partners of his or her decisions. Data driven more than ever, but simplified and focused, the bare-bone, decision-making process is a tool for the accountable, responsible manager who is enabling the drive of immediate change and immediate results. Group-manage and group-decide are things of the (ugly) past.

Organized and Respectful Environments

Ultimately, the authoritative leadership brings the long-forgotten respectful behavior, at all levels in the organization. As an antidote to the culture of entitlement we are commonly experiencing in the workforce, authoritative leadership opens the door for the culture of merit and its rewards. Chaos and confusion will give in quickly in the face of the organized structure of the formal hierarchy. The arbitration of conflicts becomes possible, as the organization recognizes the existence of conflicts and encourages employees to stand up for their beliefs.

There is also immediate attention given to issues responsible for causing strong conflicting positions, as there is a keen interest in discovering and applying the best possible solution to a challenging issue. Mechanisms preventing leader abuse, such as unfair performance appraisals and any forms of retaliation or "hate list enforcement" should be in place, with widely advertised channels and options for the employee (that is, escalation paths, investigation mechanisms, and formal processes for conflict arbitration).

If combined with formal business, the authoritative model will become successful faster, as it conveys the visual clues into knowledge, authority, and rank.

Most organizations bring in the external turnaround consultant and empower him or her to lead a department or an (important part of the) organization for (at least) the duration of the turnaround, thus making sure roadblocks are removed and execution happens without hesitation or delay. This streamlines or partially eliminates the need for leadership buy-in, and brings the authoritative leadership model to life at the same time.

Chapter 14
Documentation Planning

Documenting the steps and critical actions of a turnaround will ensure that there will be a record of changes made. Project leaders will be able to keep track of the thought process that led to the specific change. Although, in a turnaround, documentation might be the last thing on people's minds, it should be treated with just as much care as any other key piece of the restructuring action. Keeping the documentation process simple, structured, and to the point will help save time.

To design the documentation process suited for a particular turnaround plan, we need to answer a few questions:

- What are we documenting? How are we documenting it? (templates, flow charts, database)
- Where will the information be stored?
- Who is the documentation process owner?

Based on the answers, we should be able to design a streamlined process for documentation. In the case of turnarounds (ideally for all operational process changes), documentation should include the following information:

- Major process and/or policy change implemented
- Project leader
- Date of change
- Departments or business units impacted
- Reason for change
- Leadership and key stakeholder approvals sheet

- Key metrics with before and after values, goals, a two-line narrative to explain the numbers, and metrics definitions
- Before and after process-flow charts
-

With these points in mind, designing a template is quite easy. Keeping the documentation simple, concise, and to the point is important. The focus should remain on the process optimization actions rather than paperwork.

To get documentation out of our growing "to-do" list, assigning a documentation process owner is the best way to ensure changes will be properly documented. Therefore, we will add this name to the transition map presented in Chapter 4 and this person will become part of the turnaround project team. For complex turnaround plans, this resource is a team of two, consisting of one internal resource and one external—part of your turnaround consultant's support team.

What Are the Main Benefits of Documenting Process Changes?

First, it helps greatly with communication. Knowing at any time who did what and when, being able to reach out to them without hesitation in search of clarification or support with new projects are huge benefits. Being able to do a quick search in an Access database, for example, to find out what changes have been made in the returns process, will allow for quick availability of relevant data, bringing a tremendous help to any new initiatives and to understanding process behaviors.

Making sure that project leaders and process owners do not reinvent the wheel every time they look for new cost reduction opportunities is another notable benefit. This is a dual benefit, so to speak, because this also cuts back on the doubt and second-guessing that might happen when project leaders who are relatively new to the business are unsure of what has already been explored in the past. Finally, not repeating mistakes from the past is also a significant benefit.

Let's explore, using an example, how documentation can work and help you understand behaviors and fix issues.

Case Study

In our example, the company is an e-commerce business, selling music CDs. It has an in-house call center where customers call with various issues: ship status (highest number of calls), return info, product info, payment and financial questions, missing and wrong product, or damaged in transit. As part of the turnaround plan, the call center was upgraded to allow self-help through the interactive voice response (IVR). Therefore, a significant number of the calls would be handled through automation, allowing for reduction in labor and telecom costs in the call center. Another self-help section was added to the company's website. The change was implemented successfully, and the consequent reduction in call volume was documented on XPeTrack, along with the process change documentation. Here's how it looked:

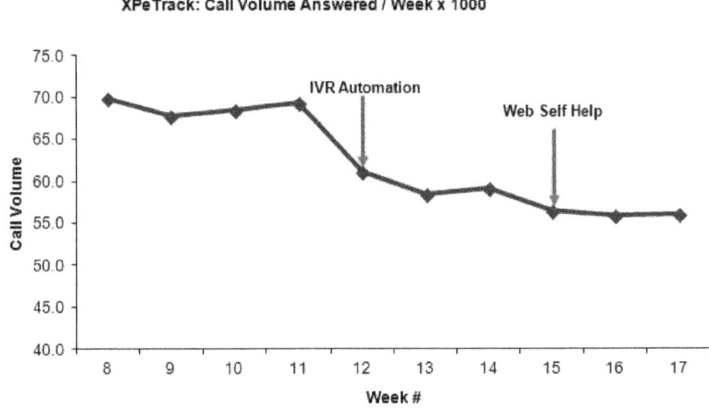

Data Points:

Week #	8	9	10	11	12	13	14	15	16	17
Call Volume Answered / week x 1000	69.9	67.8	68.5	69.4	61.2	58.5	59.1	56.5	55.9	56.1
Project 1—IVR Automation					x	x	x	x	x	x
Project 2—Web Self Help Launch								x	x	x

Fig. 14.1. XPeTrack: Call volume answered / week x 1,000.

Shown in Fig. 14.2, the process change documentation sheet reflects the change.

Two months later, the turnaround action is complete and the company is well on its way to stabilization. An initiative takes place, to brush up the voice prompt recordings in the IVR. The current recordings had been done on a crisis budget, with in-house talent, and it shows. Sometime later, after implementing the new voice prompts, and with no apparent connection, a significant upward trend in answered call volume is noted (see Fig. 14.4, data point week 18). Initially assumed as special-cause driven and temporary, after a few days it becomes obvious the increased call volume is consistent, accounting for 12–15 percent more calls each day.

Online Music for You

Process Change Documentation Sheet	
Project Name	**IVR Automation and Web Self Help Implementation for Inbound Service**
Requested by—Dept Requested by—Name: Date of Change: Project Leader—Name, Ext	Customer Service John S. Doe, VP Customer Service **IVR: 3/25—week 12** **Web Self Help: 4/15—week 15** Sam Allen
Project Description	Introducing IVR automation for 24/7 for ship status, returns info, refund info, missing, wrong & damaged in transit. Web customer care section enhancement to provide the same, plus a section with FAQs.
Reason for change: Cost, type, and code: ROI - annualized: Other benefit: KPIs Impacted:	Reduction of labor intensive call handling in favor of self help and automation $ 43,000 expense, $ 18,500 CapEx, Customer Service budget $ 525,000—labor & telecom expense 24/7 accessibility to self help service Call volume—answered
Cross-Functional Impact:	IT, Telecom, Web

Approvals

Approvals—Name Approvals—Signature Approvals—Date	John Smith, IT Director 17-Mar
Approvals—Name Approvals—Signature Approvals—Date	Jane Smith, Telecom Analyst 15-Mar
Approvals—Name Approvals—Signature Approvals—Date	Mary Jones, CTO 19-Mar

Fig. 14.2. Process change documentation sheet—initial process change.

This second project is also documented and marked on the XPeTrack, as shown in figures 14.3 and 14.4:

Online Music for You

Process Change Documentation Sheet	
Project Name	IVR Prompts Re-recording
Requested by—Dept:	Customer Service
Requested by—Name:	John S. Doe, VP Customer Service
Date of Change:	**IVR: 5/05—week 18**
Project Leader—Name, Ext	Sam Allen
Project Description	Recording all IVR prompts in a professional, studio voice.
Reason for change:	Brand Image, consistency of messaging
Cost, type and code:	$ 2,200 expense, CS budget
ROI—annualized:	soft dollar
Other benefit:	N/A
KPIs Impacted:	none
Cross-Functional Impact:	IT, Telecom, Web

Approvals

Approvals—Name	John Smith, IT Director
Approvals—Signature	
Approvals—Date	25-Apr
Approvals—Name	Jane Smith, Telecom Analyst
Approvals—Signature	
Approvals—Date	27-Apr
Approvals—Name	Mary Jones, CTO
Approvals—Signature	
Approvals—Date	30-Apr

Fig. 14.3. Process change documentation sheet—second process change.

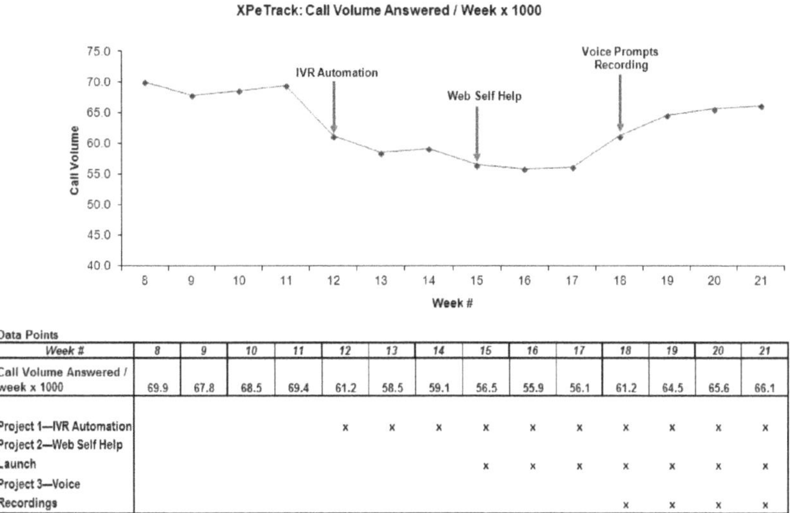

Data Points

Week #	8	9	10	11	12	13	14	15	16	17	18	19	20	21
Call Volume Answered / week x 1000	69.9	67.8	68.5	69.4	61.2	58.5	59.1	56.5	55.9	56.1	61.2	64.5	65.6	66.1
Project 1—IVR Automation					x	x	x	x	x	x	x	x	x	x
Project 2—Web Self Help Launch								x	x	x	x	x	x	x
Project 3—Voice Recordings											x	x	x	x

Fig. 14.4. XPeTrack: Call volume answered / week x 1000—after the first process change

After minimal efforts to locate the reasons behind the increased volume, it becomes apparent that the increase in volume consists of missing and wrong questions, along with product questions. At which point a lot of data analysis on product and shipping would have had to happen, but a quick look at XPeTrack for call volume was able to pinpoint with accuracy the increased call volume started precisely when the IVR prompts were rerecorded.

Pulling both IVR projects documentation files, and auditing the second project's conformity with the IVR architecture design, the team was able to identify the cause for the failure: the newly recorded prompt simply forgot to mention option 4: "For all product-related questions, press 4." Once the root cause for the failure was discovered, the fix was implemented and, just a couple of weeks and data points later, XPeTrack for offered call volume reflected the validity of the fix, in addition to the net volume being automated and the resulting financial gains.

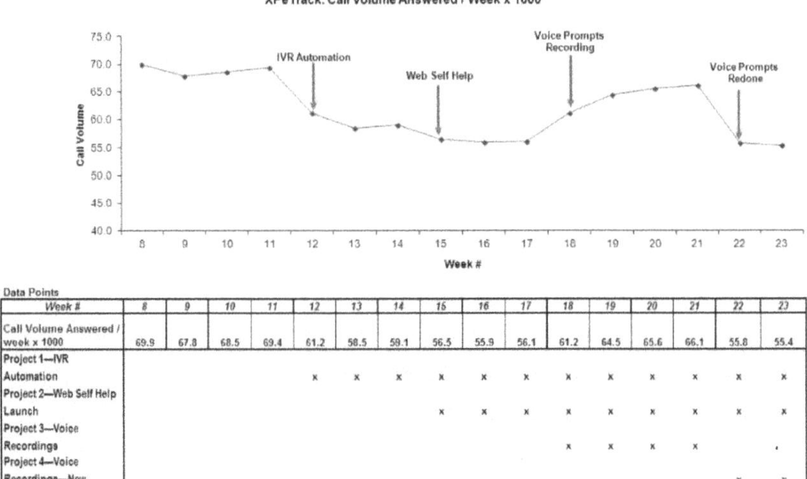

Data Points

Week #	8	9	10	11	12	13	14	15	16	17	18	19	20	21	22	23
Call Volume Answered / week x 1000	69.9	67.8	68.5	69.4	61.2	58.5	59.1	56.5	55.9	56.1	61.2	64.5	65.6	66.1	55.8	55.4
Project 1—IVR Automation					x	x	x	x	x	x	x	x	x	x	x	x
Project 2—Web Self Help Launch								x	x	x	x	x	x	x	x	x
Project 3—Voice Recordings											x	x	x	x		.
Project 4—Voice Recordings—New															x	x

Fig. 14.5. XPeTrack: Call volume answered / week x 1,000—after correcting the process error.

In our example, without proper documentation of changes made, the investigation would have taken a long time and burned through many resources. The more complex the environment, the more stringent the need to maintain proper documentation, ensure a single point of contact for all documentation and logging of all changes, and to keep the associated XPeTrack up to date.

Chapter 15
Meetings Management

Breaking the habit of back-to-back meetings is a challenge. Many organizations fall into the trap of having leadership meet in smaller or larger groups, day in and day out. Once this pattern of behavior is established within an organization, it takes a lot of coordinated effort and initiative to get the meetings calendar back to a more logical structure.

What generates the need to spend one's day in meetings? This habit is an addictive one. It represents the peak manifestation of reactive behavior at leadership level, where leaders meet because they are called into meetings and call others into meetings because that's the way things are done.

Not all meetings should be avoided. There will always be a need for people to get together in a room and discuss the issues at hand. A good, productive meeting has these features:

- An agenda that requires interaction among attendees, stating clear objectives; informative meetings can be replaced by memos and email presentations, so that everyone can absorb the information at their own pace.
- A carefully crafted attendance list.
- A documentation piece that states what was achieved, and what the next steps are—if applicable.
- A meeting leader or owner, who will make sure the agenda is followed and that all meeting objectives are met.

Therefore, this is what a good meeting looks like. Nevertheless—how many is too many? When an overcrowded meeting calendar starts interfering with the leader's ability to interact with her team, process her email, or even think, that is the unmistakable sign of too many meetings. Let's explore some of the trade-offs of the meeting addiction:

- **Unavailable to lead one's team**—in operational environments, just as in any other team environment, the presence and availability of the leader is required to guide, provide direction, and manage interference on a daily basis. The leader's unavailability generates confusion, hesitation, and delays. It also hinders the development of the leader's team members, as they learn and grow through the answers they get for questions they are asking, and through observing the leader.
- **No team building**—it's almost impossible to build a team if the leader's not present to drive it. Team building takes initiative and sustained effort, but most of all it takes time spent together.
- **No one to answer questions unless in a meeting**—whether a member of the team, or someone in another department, due to the clogged calendar of meetings and the leader's unavailability to answer her phone messages or emails, the only way to get her input is by setting up yet another meeting. Like any other addiction, this one too feeds from itself. The sad reality is that, in most cases, a question that could have been solved in five minutes or less by phone, will require at least 30 minutes set aside for the meeting; travel to and from the conference room, allowing the "possible late" time, and so on.
- **Group-think**—and its close relatives, group-decide and group-manage—are dangerous enemies of any progressive environment. There is a higher likelihood of decisions being made halfheartedly, due to the length of time it took to set up the current decision-making meeting, the number of people who all seem to agree on something you don't agree with, and how difficult it would be to even schedule a follow-up time to clarify any doubts. "Let's see . . . the earliest time everyone present has an opening to discuss this urgent matter is in . . . June?"
- **Lengthy, exhausting decision-making process**—somewhat explained above, but here is an added angle: if faced with a complex, multistep decision-making exercise, scheduling the right amount of time, in a time-efficient manner, simply cannot occur. The delays and logistical difficulties in finding the time to

set up multiple work sessions in a meeting-addicted environment will burn through any shred of passion or enthusiasm toward a decision or venture. Even the toughest, most motivated promoter of a new idea or process can become discouraged in the face of such pointless difficulties. It's called erosion. "Do I really want to push for this process change, again? Oh, well . . . whatever."

- **No ownership and accountability on decisions**—creating a culture of ownership and accountability requires an on-going, consistent push toward having decisions made by one person—the process owner. Otherwise, there is the risk of getting into the bad habit of group management. Sometimes meetings called in a meeting-addictive organization start by informing those present of a supplier issue, for example, and end up in collectively managing one particular department's organizational chart. Informing and consulting with the others? Sure. Decisions should stay, however, in the hands of the process owners, by themselves as much as possible. This might seem somewhat harsh, or "anti-team;" in reality, it is the exact opposite. If group decisions happen too often, and are replacing single-point decision making, when results are not up to expectations, the behaviors within the group will lead toward finger pointing and blame throwing. There is nothing worse at the time of a turnaround, than fostering behaviors known to lead away from top performance. Sometimes, leaders are simply not trusted to make decisions on their own, thus they are being forced into group management behaviors, as an added precaution. For those cases, there are only two reasonable alternatives: either trust them to decide, or replace them with someone who can be trusted.
- **No quick interactions**—by phone or dropping by one's office. Nothing builds the idea that a team is truly supported by its leader than finding him to be available, ready to answer questions. The best method of interaction is to "barge in," where employees from any department know he is there and they just pop in with a quick preview of tomorrow's data release, an approval for travel, a question regarding a disciplinary issue, or an idea for a new product. Soon enough, the entire office is buzzing with activity, there are no delays in finalizing tasks, and things just start happening. This is called an "open-door policy," recognized to yield immediate results in increasing productivity and team cohesion. Picking up one's phone works almost as

good. Another method is installing an online internal instant messenger (IM) system, riding on the company's email server, to allow everyone to see who is available and send questions via IM: "Are you there? Can I drop by? Have you seen the latest sales numbers? Need your input on shipping rates."

- **No time to think**—leaders should be allowed the time to think. The strategic versus tactical load should shift toward strategic and away from tactical, as the rank within the organization is higher. As seen below, the strategic load should be at or slightly under 100 percent, for director level and above; still, you will find directors who operate copiers; VPs ordering bathroom tissue and managing trivial issues, such as organizing meeting attendance or revising policy documents formatting on the Intranet.

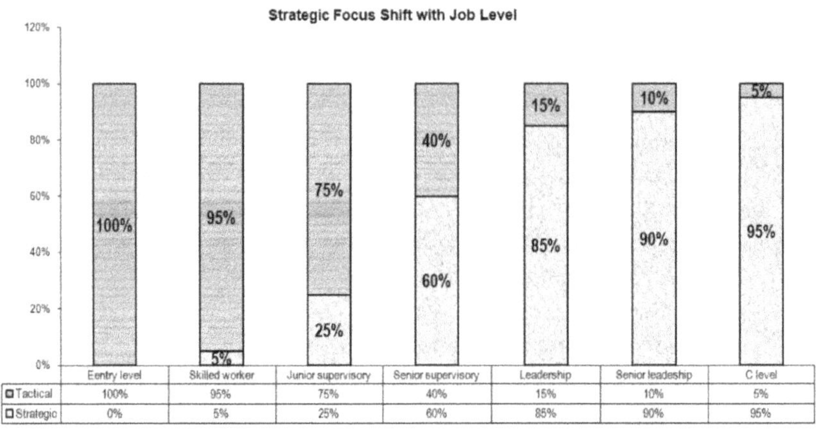

Fig. 15.1. Tactical vs. strategic focus shift with job level

Why is that? First, tactical is more comfortable to execute than strategic. Tactical is the individual comfort zone, where sinking into routine brings restful moments of peace to our weary brains. Getting out of the comfort zone requires conscious effort and time to think. If there is no time to think allowed in the daily routine of an employee with strategic workload, the strategic portion of his contribution will perish, engulfed by the tactical, easy-to-do aspects of his job, that he can squeeze with ease between tasks.

Soon enough, this turns into a 100 percent reactive behavior, where the tired leader will react to all issues in queue, solving the tactical pieces one by one, sometimes not even able to prioritize any more—just to react. He will not be able or allow himself the time to step back and be proactive—work the strategic part of the issue. Where do we want to be tomorrow, what do we want to do, so we don't keep on dealing, over and over, with the same issues? How do we need to change our current processes, so that we can have such issues addressed in a more efficient, effective manner?

Breaking the Meeting Habit

How do we break the habit of back-to-back meetings and reactive behaviors? Let's apply addiction withdrawal 101:

- **Resist the temptation**—do not click "accept" on all meeting requests. Ask for an agenda so you will know how to prepare; respond with a phone call. Do not initiate more meetings than strictly necessary. Rediscover informal, ad-hoc human interaction.
- **Fight the withdrawal symptoms**—with every cultural change, there will be resistance; any change takes effort. Educate your peers, reports, and leaders, get their buy-in—it will easier to explain to them you have a strategy—you were not just being rude for not wanting to meet with them anymore.
- **Learn to live without the bad habit**—it takes a while to reorganize and rethink your day. Nevertheless, you will discover a completely new world: one with achievements, workload finished during business hours, quality time spent with family in the evenings, and even lunch breaks.
- **Enjoy the healthy, productive life**—in which you are back in control of your professional life. Being proactive is what makes leaders become better leaders; being proactive again will feel like coming back home after a long trip in a dark place.

Chapter 16
Internal Communication

Keeping employees informed of what is going on, truthfully, openly, and timely, will help mitigate employees' fears, enroll their full support for the recovery effort, reduce turnover, and increase engagement. A comprehensive strategy is needed for the successful implementation of a communications plan, one that addresses issues freely and provides an open-conversation environment. This can prove to be a challenge, especially when balancing the confidentiality of the shared information, the timing, and target audiences, for all information packages distributed across the company, and also open question-and-answer sessions.

Let's explore some readily available employee communication channels, and their recommended uses:

Email and Voicemail Messages

Email messages are great for sharing last week's results, announce an employee sale, changes in cafeteria hours, and that is about it. Used in such a manner, email is a one-way communication vehicle and does not usually lead to or encourage dialogue. Voicemail messages recorded by senior leaders and distributed to the organization or to specific departments can be a more personal, warmer means of communication, ideal for recognizing achievements and encouraging performance and focus.

Carefully crafted messaging has to be formulated in such manner that it communicates effectively to the target audience. For example, anywhere beyond senior leadership level, acronyms like EBT and CAPEX should be replaced by the fully worded versions that will make sense to everyone. Distributed voicemail messages allow another component to contribute to the communication package: vitality and tone of voice. However, voicemail broadcast is the ultimate unidirectional communication channel.

Town Hall Meetings

They are ideal for mass-communicating impactful news to large audiences (all employees), likely to lead to arguments, disputes, or merely a high volume of questions. For example, that would be the method of choice to let employees know that the company will file for Chapter 11. At that point, the meeting leaders must be prepared with answers to any questions regarding implications of the filing, how it will affect the employees, and talking points for the customer-facing roles. It is important to keep in mind that it takes a lot of guts for an employee to stand up in the middle of a town hall meeting and voice a concern. Therefore, the meeting leader must anticipate and offer such topics. For example, this would be an approach:

> "Are we closing the doors? Absolutely not! We will continue to operate after the filing takes place. Many reputable companies have operated under bankruptcy protection, allowing them to restructure, stabilize, renegotiate terms with vendors, and increase their competitive presence on the consumer market. Chapter 11 does not mean we are closing down, selling everything, and going home. That's Chapter 7.
> And I guess you're wondering if we're able to make Friday's payroll. Yes, we are. We've already sent the payment order to the bank. Like I said before, we are continuing to operate, and that includes paying our employees. Benefits are also on your mind, I assume."

The tone of voice selected to illustrate this example was not chosen by accident. The tone and message content should stay friendly, away from business lingo, encouraging dialogue. The message explains clearly every term introduced, calls out the main concerns one by one, thus showing the employees the willingness to discuss openly, and making sure all key areas of interest are touched with clarification.

The meeting leader should also offer the option to have different functional leaders take the floor—if particular questions should arise. For instance, a plant manager might be best to answer product quality concerns, or the financial officer can answer stock market and shares performance questions.

Two secondary communication tools support such important communication, after the fact: the employee hotline and the Intranet. To ensure the availability of essential parts of the messaging, while going into enough level of detail, after the town meeting has been adjourned, introducing an employee hotline is a quick, inexpensive way to avoid a wave of questions aimed at certain areas of the organization: HR, benefits, and payroll. The same type of messaging should be reflected on the company's Intranet. Both the hotline and the Intranet channels can have unidirectional or bidirectional applications. For example, for the hotline, there can be an automated messaging structure addressing with prerecorded voice the key issues that would most likely need addressing. It can also have a mailbox function, in which callers can leave messages and requests for callbacks with further clarifications, if needed.

Anonymous "Ask Us" Box

Despite all best efforts of the leadership to encourage employees to voice their concerns, some might still feel unsafe to do so in an open manner, especially when layoffs are in the air. To address these concerns, which otherwise might never surface, "Ask Us" boxes can be provided, where employees can insert notes with questions. Once a week—or however frequently we might choose—a dedicated team or individual will open the box and answer all the questions received, sending the document with questions and answers to the entire organization. There are two key points to remember:

- All questions must be answered, regardless of how uncomfortable or how non-business related. An organization cannot be perceived to be censoring the questions from employees. Sometimes, a question such as "What makes the world turn?" responded with "Money," will make everyone smile and relax a notch. Quite useful during times of hardship.
- The tone must be a careful balance between optimistic and serious. Someone once said, "I am starting to feel bipolar. Each day we get a rah-rah communication, followed two hours later by a memo advising we have a cash shortage requiring

immediate action." Balance, stability, and consistency of messaging become critical.

Communication Strategy Design

A good communication strategy will have clear milestones, complete with communication packages defined by answering these questions:

- Who and where is the audience? Internal vs. external, companywide vs. departmental, etc.
- What communication channel(s) will we use? (that is, email, town hall, etc.).
- What needs to be communicated? What is the key message? What are we trying to achieve?
- Is the communication confidential? Until when? (that is, not announcing companywide the bankruptcy filing until after market close the day prior). If needed, insert a confidentiality note.
- What should the general tone of the message be?
- What is the anticipated reaction?

In the case of a turnaround, communication is critically important to ensure that employees will remain on board and committed to make the turnaround action a success. A consistent, comprehensive, two-way communication strategy will help with the retention of key contributors.

Therefore, the issues that communication should not omit to address are mainly the issues that would lead employees to start looking for work elsewhere:

1. Issues with impact to the employee's livelihood, job security, and income
    - Reduced hours
    - Benefits
    - Severance
    - Layoffs
    - Potential bankruptcy filing, implications, strategy, etc.
2. Issues with impact to the employee's career, engagement, and future development
    - Performance and KPIs
    - Goals and objectives, alignment

- Bonuses

3. Issues with impact to the employee's perception of the company, its financial health its future
    - Planning, sales quotas, and results
    - Stock and financial markets questions—price of shares, trading, etc.
    - Potential changes in control
    - Strategy / vision pre- and post-turnaround
    - Economy and industry forecasting

Caveats in Communication

Finally, there are a few caveats in employee communication:

- **Sounding false.** There's nothing more damaging to employees' trust and confidence in the leadership's ability to turn the company around, than hearing them avoid calling things by their name, recognizing limitations, sounding falsely positive, or deceptive.
- **Not acknowledging errors made in the recent past.** The employees' level of confidence with leadership requires errors to be acknowledged and owned, especially those widely known, blatant ones, that have caused financial or other type of damage. Part of the error acknowledgment should be a plan to correct the error, complete with deadlines and goals. Otherwise, employees might assume the flawed thinking is continuing, and the errors will keep appearing. An example of a good way to convey the correct message could be, "Following years of constant success, we have opened new dealer locations in an accelerated manner, at a time when the economy is on a downturn. This, unfortunately, did not prove to be the best thing to do. Going forward, we are reassessing the profitability of these new locations, and we will take immediate action to bring these locations back to the black."
- **Having a pep rally without basis.** Two good sales days do not constitute a trend. Celebrating too soon, followed by the disappointment of another bad run, is more damaging to employee morale than no action at all.
- **Transmitting the image of lack of focus or alignment at leadership level.** Leadership should align on content, tone, and purpose on all communication before proceeding.

- **Not committing to dates and deliverables.** This makes communication sound fake. A date is critical for this phrase, "By April 15th, the results of our direct marketing campaign will have compensated the losses of Q1." If we cannot commit to a date, then we should be replacing it with a phrase showing commitment to achieve results fast. "We have launched an aggressive direct marketing campaign, and we will be communicating the results as soon as they are in. We are confident it will help us mitigate the losses of Q1."
- **Not having clear talking points for customer—or public—facing roles**. The last thing you'd want to have is a sales rep freely speculate with a consumer—or even worse, a reporter—on the likelihood of the company maintaining its warranty commitment in case of a bankruptcy filing. Public relations experts, in cooperation with leaders of the customer-facing departments, should develop these talking points.

Stage 2
Execution

"It's not enough that we do our best; sometimes we have to do what's required."

~Sir Winston Churchill (1874–1965)

Chapter 17
Right-Sizing the Organization

The time has come for the tough decisions to turn into action. Although restructuring might seem to be the obvious solution for any money-losing organization, restructuring can be planned and executed in many ways—not all efficient. Finding the right strategy for your business might pose a bit of a challenge, so we will examine the most common strategies, and explore the situations for which they make most sense.

To do that, we will use the example introduced in Chapter 4, reiterated below to refresh our memory: EXPL Inc., the multi-dealership car sales business.

Case Study

> Last year, EXPL Inc. posted a loss of $37M, with sales revenue of $550M. For this year, the forecasts show a much steeper decline in sales, down to $396M. Unless significant action is taken, the company will run out of cash in little over six months. EXPL Inc. is in the car sales business, with 38 dealerships nationwide. The industry is in a lot of trouble and forecasts are grim.

In Chapter 4, we explored the planning aspect of the organizational redesign of EXPL Inc., and we were able to put together the high-level turnaround transition map. After our last revision, it looked like this:

EXPL—Current Org	EXPL—Future Design	Key Actions	Owner(s)
Headoffice overhead @ $12M	Headoffice overhead @ $4.9M	Reduce management headcount, redesign org, outsource backoffice functions	Jones (Stevens, Corey, Smith, Johnson)
Dealership count: 38	Dealership count: 16	Identify low performing locations and close; reassign / liquidate inventory	Adams (Benson, Evans, McDonnel)
-	Online sales division	Create, implement, staff	Samuel (Jameson, Schmidt)
In-house printing operation	-	Outsource	Johnson
Dealership level organization	Optimized, increased variability	Reduced fixed headcount, reassign tasks towards variable	Matthews (Stevens, Foley)
Inventory $72M	Inventory @ $30M	Organize close-out sales events, heavy promo, sell at cost	Trenton (Peterson, Phelps, Ricks)
Project Manager: Chris Jackson (XYZ Consulting)			
Documentation: Julie Anderson (x 5355), Annie Smithe (XYZ Consulting)			

Fig. 17.1. Turnaround action planning—transition map, with owners and teams.

The challenge was to build an organization that would be profitable at $396M sales revenue, and to position it for future growth.

The rule of thumb in such cases is to take the percentage of the revenue drop and apply it as an expenses-reduction goal. For instance, EXPL Inc. has dropped revenue from $973M (two years ago was its last profitable year) to $396M (this year's forecast); therefore, it dropped by 60 percent. Sales revenue this year is expected to be only 40 percent of what it was two years ago. Therefore, quite logically, expenses should drop by roughly the same percentage to ensure survival. This is, in fact, how we came out with the number of dealerships to be kept in the future organization: 16 is roughly 40 percent of 38.

This is a rule of thumb for a reason: it guides the thinking in terms of size of the reduction in cost. It is also an approximation, which does not take into consideration other issues, such as brand presence in certain areas, lease agreements, penalties, etc. Therefore, at the end of the exercise, we might decide we want to keep more than 16 dealerships; the balance of expense needs to be covered from other sources, if that would end up being the case.

To keep things simple for our case study, we will consider all things were created equal and there were no considerations at this point leading us away from the 60 percent drop in cost across the board. The next question is how do we select the locations to be closed? Of course, based on results. For any such decisions, to ensure the list is built in a manner that would yield the maximum benefit possible for the business, the method of choice is to rank the locations, based on a number of productivity and profitability criteria.

A recommended methodology for such a complex decision is XPeRank (for Expedient Ranking). XPeRank is a methodology for selecting a part of a group of many similar units (that is, workers as part of a team, retail store locations as part of a chain store, bolts as part of a bolts lot of many similar bolts, etc.), based on the combination of multiple performance and/or characteristics criteria. Let us work through an XPeRank exercise, using EXPL Inc. and its 38 locations as an example.

Methodology—XPeRank

Step 1: Establish the key indicators for the ranking. It can be more than one, but they need to have comparable strength or be weighted appropriately. The key indicator should be, for now, monthly average revenue—for the past three months. It looks like this:

Monthly Revenue By Location		
Location ID	Monthly Revenue (M)	
1	$	1.13
2	$	1.15
3	$	0.53
4	$	0.38
5	$	0.27
6	$	0.47
7	$	1.08
8	$	0.54
9	$	0.43
10	$	1.04
11	$	1.05
12	$	0.38
13	$	0.85
14	$	0.74
15	$	1.00
16	$	0.81
17	$	0.89
18	$	1.12
19	$	1.23
20	$	1.11
21	$	0.91
22	$	1.77
23	$	1.68
24	$	1.27
25	$	0.43
26	$	0.65
27	$	0.85
28	$	0.89
29	$	1.24
30	$	1.06
31	$	1.13
32	$	1.11
33	$	0.76
34	$	0.61
35	$	1.11
36	$	0.36
37	$	0.65
38	$	0.45
Total	**$**	**33.10**

Fig.17.2. Dealership locations with monthly average revenue ($M).
Step 2: Ranking the locations based on the monthly revenue.

Considering that the higher the revenue, the better—reorganizes the list and adds a ranking to each location:

	XPeRank—Revenue		
	Location ID	Monthly Revenue (M)	Sales Ranking
*	22	$ 1.77	1
*	23	$ 1.68	2
*	24	$ 1.27	3
*	29	$ 1.24	4
*	19	$ 1.23	5
*	2	$ 1.15	6
*	31	$ 1.13	7
*	1	$ 1.12	8
*	18	$ 1.12	9
*	35	$ 1.11	10
*	20	$ 1.11	12
*	32	$ 1.11	11
*	7	$ 1.08	13
*	30	$ 1.06	14
*	11	$ 1.05	15
*	10	$ 1.04	16
	15	$ 0.99	17
	21	$ 0.91	18
	28	$ 0.89	19
	17	$ 0.89	20
	13	$ 0.85	21
	27	$ 0.85	22
	16	$ 0.81	23
	33	$ 0.76	24
	14	$ 0.74	25
	37	$ 0.65	26
	26	$ 0.65	27
	34	$ 0.61	28
	8	$ 0.54	29
	3	$ 0.53	30
	6	$ 0.47	31
	38	$ 0.44	32
	25	$ 0.43	33
	9	$ 0.43	34
	4	$ 0.38	36
	12	$ 0.38	35
	36	$ 0.36	37
	5	$ 0.27	38
	Total	**$ 33.08**	

Fig.17.3. Dealership locations ranked by monthly average revenue ($M).

It was easy to draw the line just under location ranking 16. But there are a few takeaways we need to consider:

1. Removing a location removes its revenue. What percentage of the lost revenue will be redirected to other locations, and what will be lost to the competition?
2. Can we afford to close these locations? We need to examine the costs associated with shutting them down.
3. Are there any strategically important locations or other considerations that we need to keep in mind?

Number 1 is a complex question, with answers varying from location to location depending on proximity to alternate locations, traffic numbers, and other considerations. The individual answers must be carefully forecast, not overstated—as it would lead to further operating losses. Numbers 2 and 3 require that we add more key indicators and rankings, before making any decisions. Let us proceed.

Step 3: Adding a second ranking criterion. The next one to add is location performance, calculated as earnings before tax (EBT), and its ranking—the higher, the better.

The revised ranking table is illustrated in Fig. 17.4. Lines shown with an asterisk to their left represent locations that, based solely on the revenue ranking, would have stayed open:

XPeRank—Revenue and EBT

	Location ID	Monthly Revenue (M)	Sales Ranking	Expenses (M)	EBT (M)	EBT Ranking
*	22	$ 1.77	1	$ 1.02	$ 0.75	1
*	23	$ 1.68	2	$ 1.11	$ 0.57	2
*	29	$ 1.24	4	$ 0.67	$ 0.57	3
	34	$ 0.61	28	$ 0.46	$ 0.16	4
	3	$ 0.53	30	$ 0.40	$ 0.13	5
	8	$ 0.54	29	$ 0.42	$ 0.12	6
	9	$ 0.43	34	$ 0.31	$ 0.12	7
	36	$ 0.36	37	$ 0.26	$ 0.10	8
	14	$ 0.74	25	$ 0.65	$ 0.09	9
	37	$ 0.65	26	$ 0.57	$ 0.09	10
	12	$ 0.38	35	$ 0.31	$ 0.07	11
*	7	$ 1.08	13	$ 1.01	$ 0.07	12
	25	$ 0.43	33	$ 0.38	$ 0.06	13
	38	$ 0.45	32	$ 0.45	$ 0.00	14
*	1	$ 1.13	8	$ 1.13	$ (0.00)	15
	15	$ 1.00	17	$ 1.00	$ (0.00)	16
*	10	$ 1.04	16	$ 1.09	$ (0.05)	17
*	2	$ 1.15	6	$ 1.23	$ (0.08)	18
	4	$ 0.38	36	$ 0.47	$ (0.09)	19
	6	$ 0.47	31	$ 0.57	$ (0.10)	20
*	20	$ 1.11	12	$ 1.21	$ (0.10)	21
*	11	$ 1.05	15	$ 1.16	$ (0.11)	22
*	31	$ 1.13	7	$ 1.26	$ (0.13)	23
*	32	$ 1.11	11	$ 1.24	$ (0.13)	24
*	30	$ 1.06	14	$ 1.22	$ (0.16)	25
	27	$ 0.85	22	$ 1.04	$ (0.19)	26
	5	***$ 0.27***	***38***	***$ 0.46***	***$ (0.19)***	***27***
	13	$ 0.85	21	$ 1.05	$ (0.20)	28
	33	***$ 0.76***	***24***	***$ 1.02***	***$ (0.26)***	***29***
*	35	$ 1.11	10	$ 1.42	$ (0.31)	30
	21	$ 0.91	18	$ 1.22	$ (0.31)	31
	17	$ 0.89	20	$ 1.22	$ (0.33)	32
*	18	$ 1.12	9	$ 1.46	$ (0.34)	33
	26	$ 0.65	27	$ 1.02	$ (0.37)	34
	28	$ 0.89	19	$ 1.29	$ (0.40)	35
*	24	$ 1.27	3	$ 1.77	$ (0.50)	36
	16	$ 0.81	23	$ 1.36	$ (0.55)	37
*	19	$ 1.23	5	$ 1.82	$ (0.59)	38
	Total	$ 33.09			$ (2.63)	

Fig.17.4. Dealership locations with two ranking criteria: revenue and EBT.

A few notable surprises can be seen:

- Many of the high-volume locations are not profitable. Keeping them will not make the problem go away. There is an opportunity to restructure at location level.
- Locations ranking 1, 2, and 4 for sales volume, also rank 1, 2, and 3 for EBT. Their operational model is a winner—should be applied immediately in all underperforming locations. Those location managers (units 22, 29, and 23) should become part of the turnaround team. They can share valuable, proven knowledge and experience.
- Based on this analysis, the sales revenue for the year is trending toward $397M, while EBT is heading for a negative $19M (head office excluded).
- Locations 5 and 33—marked in bold and italic font—have been deemed strategically important, so they cannot be closed.

Step 4: Initial recommendations: Based on these findings, we are ready to prepare our initial recommendations, considering both the revenue ranking and the EBT ranking. Rather than pure data, in this simple example we will use a combination of data and decision-making convention, as follows:

- Positive EBT locations will stay open.
- Negative EBT locations will be restructured IF they rank among the first 16 from a revenue perspective (marked with an asterisk), or IF their losses are minimal.
- Low revenue, negative EBT locations will close.

Applying these criteria, here is the initial list of recommendations:

	XPeRank—Revenue and EBT										
	Location ID	Monthly Revenue (M)		Sales Ranking	Expenses (M)		EBT (M)		EBT Ranking	Recommended Action
*	22	$	1.77	1	$	1.02	$	0.75	1	Stays Open
*	23	$	1.68	2	$	1.11	$	0.57	2	Stays Open
*	29	$	1.24	4	$	0.67	$	0.57	3	Stays Open
	34	$	0.61	28	$	0.46	$	0.16	4	Stays Open
	3	$	0.53	30	$	0.40	$	0.13	5	Stays Open
	8	$	0.54	29	$	0.42	$	0.12	6	Stays Open
	9	$	0.43	34	$	0.31	$	0.12	7	Stays Open
	36	$	0.36	37	$	0.26	$	0.10	8	Stays Open
	14	$	0.74	25	$	0.65	$	0.09	9	Stays Open
	37	$	0.65	26	$	0.57	$	0.09	10	Stays Open
	12	$	0.38	35	$	0.31	$	0.07	11	Stays Open
*	7	$	1.08	13	$	1.01	$	0.07	12	Stays Open
	25	$	0.43	33	$	0.38	$	0.06	13	Stays Open
	38	$	0.45	32	$	0.45	$	0.00	14	Restructure - Make Profitable
*	1	$	1.13	8	$	1.13	$	(0.00)	15	Restructure - Make Profitable
	15	$	1.00	17	$	1.00	$	(0.00)	16	Restructure - Make Profitable
*	10	$	1.04	16	$	1.09	$	(0.05)	17	Restructure - Make Profitable
*	2	$	1.15	6	$	1.23	$	(0.08)	18	Restructure - Make Profitable
	4	$	0.38	36	$	0.47	$	(0.09)	19	Close
	6	$	0.47	31	$	0.57	$	(0.10)	20	Close
*	20	$	1.11	12	$	1.21	$	(0.10)	21	Restructure - Make Profitable
*	11	$	1.05	15	$	1.16	$	(0.11)	22	Restructure - Make Profitable
*	31	$	1.13	7	$	1.26	$	(0.13)	23	Restructure - Make Profitable
*	32	$	1.11	11	$	1.24	$	(0.13)	24	Restructure - Make Profitable
*	30	$	1.06	14	$	1.22	$	(0.16)	25	Restructure - Make Profitable
	27	$	0.85	22	$	1.04	$	(0.19)	26	Close
	5	**$**	**0.27**	**38**	**$**	**0.46**	**$**	**(0.19)**	**27**	***Restructure - Make Profitable***
	13	$	0.85	21	$	1.05	$	(0.20)	28	Close
	33	**$**	**0.76**	**24**	**$**	**1.02**	**$**	**(0.26)**	**29**	***Restructure - Make Profitable***
*	35	$	1.11	10	$	1.42	$	(0.31)	30	Restructure - Make Profitable
	21	$	0.91	18	$	1.22	$	(0.31)	31	Close
	17	$	0.89	20	$	1.22	$	(0.33)	32	Close
*	18	$	1.12	9	$	1.46	$	(0.34)	33	Restructure - Make Profitable
	26	$	0.65	27	$	1.02	$	(0.37)	34	Close
	28	$	0.89	19	$	1.29	$	(0.40)	35	Close
*	24	$	1.27	3	$	1.77	$	(0.50)	36	Restructure - Make Profitable
	16	$	0.81	23	$	1.36	$	(0.55)	37	Close
*	19	$	1.23	5	$	1.82	$	(0.59)	38	Restructure - Make Profitable
	Total	**$**	**33.09**				**$**	**(2.63)**		

Fig.17.5. Initial recommendations based on three decision-making conventions.

The exceptions are:

- Numbers 5 and 33—we restructure instead of close them, due to strategic importance.
- Numbers 38 and 15—we restructure, due to the small size of the loss; turning the units around should not pose too much of a challenge.

The recommendations were based on these rules:

- If a unit is making money, keep it open.
- If a unit is losing money, but it ranked high in the sales revenue (above initial cutoff line), keep it open, but turn it around to profitability.
- If a unit is losing money and it ranked under the sales volume cutoff line, it should be closed.

Step 5: Usually required for more complex analyses. This last step provides another way to reach a consistent decision based on data ranking: by adding the ranking points and generating a list. It's also a good way to verify the judgment and decisions were correct; in our case, instead of reworking the recommendations based on added ranking points, we'll just reorder the list based on the ranking points and see how the recommendations line up:

	XPeRank—Revenue and EBT							
	Location ID	Monthly Revenue (M)	Sales Ranking	Expenses (M)	EBT (M)	EBT Ranking	Rank 1+2	Recommended Action
*	22	$ 1.77	1	$ 1.02	$ 0.75	1	2	Stays Open
*	23	$ 1.68	2	$ 1.11	$ 0.57	2	4	Stays Open
*	29	$ 1.24	4	$ 0.67	$ 0.57	3	7	Stays Open
*	1	$ 1.13	8	$ 1.13	$ -	15	23	Restructure - Make Profitable
*	2	$ 1.15	6	$ 1.23	$ (0.08)	18	24	Restructure - Make Profitable
*	7	$ 1.08	13	$ 1.01	$ 0.07	12	25	Stays Open
*	31	$ 1.13	7	$ 1.26	$ (0.13)	23	30	Restructure - Make Profitable
	34	$ 0.61	28	$ 0.46	$ 0.16	4	32	Stays Open
	15	$ 1.00	17	$ 1.00	$ -	16	33	Restructure - Make Profitable
*	10	$ 1.04	16	$ 1.09	$ (0.05)	17	33	Restructure - Make Profitable
*	20	$ 1.11	12	$ 1.21	$ (0.10)	21	33	Restructure - Make Profitable
	14	$ 0.74	25	$ 0.65	$ 0.09	9	34	Stays Open
	3	$ 0.53	30	$ 0.40	$ 0.13	5	35	Stays Open
	8	$ 0.54	29	$ 0.42	$ 0.12	6	35	Stays Open
*	32	$ 1.11	11	$ 1.24	$ (0.13)	24	35	Restructure - Make Profitable
	37	$ 0.65	26	$ 0.57	$ 0.09	10	36	Stays Open
*	11	$ 1.05	15	$ 1.16	$ (0.11)	22	37	Restructure - Make Profitable
*	30	$ 1.06	14	$ 1.22	$ (0.16)	25	39	Restructure - Make Profitable
*	24	$ 1.27	3	$ 1.77	$ (0.50)	36	39	Restructure - Make Profitable
*	35	$ 1.11	10	$ 1.42	$ (0.31)	30	40	Restructure - Make Profitable
	9	$ 0.43	34	$ 0.31	$ 0.12	7	41	Stays Open
*	18	$ 1.12	9	$ 1.46	$ (0.34)	33	42	Restructure - Make Profitable
*	19	$ 1.23	5	$ 1.82	$ (0.59)	38	43	Restructure - Make Profitable
	36	$ 0.36	37	$ 0.26	$ 0.10	8	45	Stays Open
	12	$ 0.38	35	$ 0.31	$ 0.07	11	46	Stays Open
	25	$ 0.43	33	$ 0.38	$ 0.06	13	46	Stays Open
	38	$ 0.45	32	$ 0.45	$ 0.00	14	46	Restructure - Make Profitable
	27	$ 0.85	22	$ 1.04	$ (0.19)	26	48	Close
	13	$ 0.85	21	$ 1.05	$ (0.20)	28	49	Close
	21	$ 0.91	18	$ 1.22	$ (0.31)	31	49	Close
	6	$ 0.47	31	$ 0.57	$ (0.10)	20	51	Close
	17	$ 0.89	20	$ 1.22	$ (0.33)	32	52	Close
	33	***$ 0.76***	***24***	***$ 1.02***	***$ (0.26)***	***29***	***53***	***Restructure - Make Profitable***
	28	$ 0.89	19	$ 1.29	$ (0.40)	35	54	Close
	4	$ 0.38	36	$ 0.47	$ (0.09)	19	55	Close
	16	$ 0.81	23	$ 1.36	$ (0.55)	37	60	Close
	26	$ 0.65	27	$ 1.02	$ (0.37)	34	61	Close
	5	***$ 0.27***	***38***	***$ 0.46***	***$ (0.19)***	***27***	***65***	***Restructure - Make Profitable***
	Total	**$ 33.10**			**$ (2.63)**			

Fig.17.6. Initial recommendations based on multiple ranking score.

It's interesting to notice that there is a clear cutoff line under which all our "close" recommendations fall, except for the exceptions of 5 and 33. Your turnaround consultant would also come with recommendations as to how much time should be allowed for the unit level turnarounds; in our particular example, there isn't any time so there would be a three-month restructuring period, after which the locations that are not back in the black financially will have to close.

Additional exceptions from this list of recommendations will happen in the cases where the cost to close will either not be affordable at the time of the turnaround, or will pose a big enough challenge to warrant the exception and attempt to turn the location around, despite the size of its losses.

In conclusion, we have decided to close only nine locations, to start with. The issue should be revisited for the 16 locations marked "Restructure—Make Profitable," after allowing them the time and resources to turn around.

This approach has a number of advantages: it is completely data driven, positions the company for future growth, minimizes the cash impact of a large number of location closures, and engages the use of internal resources, knowledge, and expertise (managers of units 22, 23, and 29) to help turn things around.

Chapter 18
Executing Layoffs

Layoffs are challenging for everyone: for the leaders who must decide who stays and who goes, for the employees impacted, and even for those who will survive the cut but are doomed to live in the fear of termination and in the gloomy atmosphere that encompasses layoffs in any organization. Layoff execution needs to avoid becoming either an opportunity for managers' favoritism, or an opportunity to execute on managers' hate lists. Therefore, layoff execution needs to be, as with any other critical decision, a data-driven decision, guided by clear criteria and rules, with no exceptions.

Using a similar strategy as the one used to determine which EXPL locations were to be closed, we need to decide on individual critical key metrics for each business unit in need to execute reductions in force. Therefore, using a manufacturing example this time, we will apply the XPeRank methodology to rank 15 employees, based on multiple criteria, derived from a balanced scorecard set of metrics. We will use those metrics that make the most impact on the company's survival; we call those metrics "critical to survival."

This will enable the business to be successful after the turnaround action is complete, ensuring the staff retained is the best from all perspectives: productivity, quality of work, and reliability. In our example, these are number of units produced per day, quality control score, and attendance score. For a ranking based on the first two metrics selected to be relevant and fair, the units have to be of equal complexity and duration to execute; in short, the selected metrics have to differentiate the workers based on their skills and abilities, in a fair, consistent manner.

We have decided to look at their average performance over an extended period of time—three months, in our example—to make sure we do not draw conclusions based on special cause data: time off, sick days, episodic low performance due to personal or environmental issues, or potential learning curves.

Now we will rank our employees based on each of these metrics—for each metric, we will insert a rank, listing the best performance as top ranking in the respective metric category. Following the same thought process as we did in the previous chapter, we add the rankings for each employee, thus obtaining a final ranking score. This score will allow a quick sort based on their balanced performance. Then, we are drawing the line at a particular level in our list as dictated by the size of the reduction in workforce that we need to implement. In our example, we need to cut 60 percent of the workforce, so the line will be drawn under employee 6 in our performance-ranked list.

Methodology:
XPeRank for a Team of 15 Workers

Step 1: Based on a three-month average of number of identical units produced by day, our list of employees looks like this:

XPeRank—Productivity	
Employee ID	**Productivity Units per Day 3 mo avg.**
2111	14
2105	13
2106	22
2103	25
2101	25
2114	19
2102	29
2104	16
2110	17
2108	27
2100	13
2109	12
2107	18
2113	17
2112	12

Fig. 18.1. Employees with monthly average productivity results.

Step 2: Sorting the list descending by productivity, and introducing the productivity ranking, most productive employee ranked first, the list becomes as shown in Fig. 18.2.

In case of a tie—for equal results, we assign equal ranking, and skip one spot. More precisely, two workers who tie at 13 units per day both receive rank 12, but rank 13 does not exist anymore.

XPeRank—Productivity		
Employee ID	Productivity Units per Day, 3 mo. avg.	Productivity Ranking
2102	29	1
2108	27	2
2103	25	4
2101	25	3
2106	22	5
2114	19	6
2107	18	7
2110	17	8
2113	17	8
2104	16	10
2111	14	11
2105	13	12
2100	13	12
2109	12	14
2112	12	14

Fig. 18.2. Employees with productivity ranking.

Step 3: In the same way, we are adding the second and third metrics, and rank the employees based on each of them, using the same convention: best performer ranks first. The quality score ranking is shown in Fig. 18.3.

XPeRank—Quality Score		
Employee ID	Quality Score, 3 mo. avg.	Quality Ranking
2111	99.85%	1
2113	98.31%	2
2110	98.23%	3
2107	97.77%	4
2103	97.70%	5
2106	97.59%	6
2114	97.53%	7
2104	97.36%	8
2101	97.34%	9
2105	96.96%	10
2108	96.91%	11
2112	95.95%	12
2109	95.37%	13
2100	95.15%	14
2102	95.02%	15

Fig. 18.3. Employees with quality ranking.

Next, comes the attendance ranking. In this case, the lowest average lateness minutes per month ranks the highest.

XPeRank—Attendance		
Employee ID	Attendance Mins Late per Month, 3 mo. avg.	Attendance Ranking
2111	3	1
2113	8	2
2112	10	3
2107	16	4
2106	20	5
2110	23	6
2104	32	7
2109	39	8
2103	49	9
2100	67	10
2108	76	11
2101	77	12
2105	90	13
2102	106	14
2114	115	15

Fig. 18.4. Employees with attendance ranking.

Step 4: We now add the ranking points, and resort the list based on the total ranking points column.

XPeRank—all criteria							
Employee ID	Productivity Units per Day, 3 mo. avg.	Productivity Ranking	Quality Score, 3 mo. avg.	Quality Ranking	Attendance Mins Late per Month, 3 mo. avg.	Attendance Ranking	Total Ranking
2113	17	8	98.31%	2	8	2	12
2111	14	11	99.85%	1	3	1	13
2107	18	7	97.77%	4	16	4	15
2106	22	5	97.59%	6	20	5	16
2110	17	8	98.23%	3	23	6	17
2103	25	4	97.70%	5	49	9	18
2108	27	2	96.91%	11	76	11	24
2101	25	3	97.34%	9	77	12	24
2104	16	10	97.36%	8	32	7	25
2114	19	6	97.53%	7	115	15	28
2112	12	14	95.95%	12	10	3	29
2102	29	1	95.02%	15	106	14	30
2109	12	14	95.37%	13	39	8	35
2105	13	12	96.96%	10	90	13	35
2100	13	12	95.15%	14	67	10	36

Fig. 18.5. Employees with all criteria and combined ranking points, equal weight criteria.

Resorting the list by total ranking will rank the employees based on their overall performance: productivity, quality, and attendance. Drawing the line under the sixth ranked employee will indicate those who will be on the layoff list. We see that two pairs of employees are tied (highlighted in Fig. 18.5)—total ranking points 24 and 35. However, both tied pairs will fall under the line. If this would not have happened, in cases of a tie, tenure can be used to differentiate.

	XPeRank—All Criteria							
	Employee ID	Productivity Units per Day, 3 mo. avg.	*Productivity Ranking*	Quality Score, 3 mo. avg.	Quality Ranking	Attendance Mins Late per Month, 3 mo. avg.	Attendance Ranking	Total Ranking
*	2113	17	8	98.31%	2	8	2	12
*	2111	14	11	99.85%	1	3	1	13
*	2107	18	7	97.77%	4	16	4	15
*	2106	22	5	97.59%	6	20	5	16
*	2110	17	8	98.23%	3	23	6	17
*	2103	25	4	97.70%	5	49	9	18
	2108	27	2	96.91%	11	76	11	24
	2101	25	3	97.34%	9	77	12	24
	2104	16	10	97.36%	8	32	7	25
	2114	19	6	97.53%	7	115	15	28
	2112	12	14	95.95%	12	10	3	29
	2102	29	1	95.02%	15	106	14	30
	2109	12	14	95.37%	13	39	8	35
	2105	13	12	96.96%	10	90	13	35
	2100	13	12	95.15%	14	67	10	36

Fig. 18.6. Top performing employees selected using combined ranking points, equal weight criteria.

In our example, the decision to use multiple criteria for selection used an equally weighted approach. In some cases, leaders might feel that productivity is three times more important, or relevant, than attendance. In such cases, the various weights of each metric can be reflected in the total ranking, by applying a weight factor to the contributing ranking points.

Using the same data, we will consider that productivity weighs 60 percent, quality 30 percent, and attendance the remaining 10 percent. The total ranking formula becomes:

Total Ranking = (Productivity Ranking * 60 percent + Quality Ranking * 30 percent + Attendance Ranking * 10 percent) * 100

	XPeRank—Weighted Criteria							
	Employee ID	Productivity Units per Day, 3 mo. avg.	Productivity Ranking	Quality Score, 3 mo. avg.	Quality Ranking	Attendance Mins Late per Month, 3 mo. avg.	Attendance Ranking	Total Ranking
		Weight: 60%		Weight: 30%		Weight: 10%		
*	2103	25	4	97.70%	5	49	9	480
*	2106	22	5	97.59%	6	20	5	530
*	2113	17	8	98.31%	2	8	2	560
	2108	27	2	96.91%	11	76	11	560
	2101	25	3	97.34%	9	77	12	570
*	2107	18	7	97.77%	4	16	4	580
*	2110	17	8	98.23%	3	23	6	630
	2102	29	1	95.02%	15	106	14	650
*	2111	14	11	99.85%	1	3	1	700
	2114	19	6	97.53%	7	115	15	720
	2104	16	10	97.36%	8	32	7	910
	2105	13	12	96.96%	10	90	13	1150
	2112	12	14	95.95%	12	10	3	1230
	2100	13	12	95.15%	14	67	10	1240
	2109	12	14	95.37%	13	39	8	1310

Fig. 18.7. Top performing employees selected using combined ranking points, weighted criteria.

The employees who had made the cut with equally weighted criteria are marked with an asterisk on the left. After sorting by total weighted ranking, we see that only four of them are above the line.

In some cases, it is recommended to look at performance ratings before doing the multiple ranking exercise. If performance is managed correctly within an organization, has clear KPIs, a dispute resolution process with escalation paths, and a formal review process, it would be recommended to apply the reduction in workforce starting with the "does not meet expectations" employees, and ranking those who were "meets expectations" for the previous reporting period. However, if the performance review and goal-setting processes are not formalized, consistent, or fair, and reviews are more or less given on a subjective basis, using reviews as a basis for selecting layoff list names can lead to legal exposure.

More on formalized goal setting and performance reviews will be discussed in Chapters 25 and 26.

When executing layoffs, there are a few important things to keep in mind:

Communication

There is nothing worse than news of layoffs that leak before the official communication is executed, or people who hear they have lost their jobs in a hallway or through a restroom wall. Layoffs have to be planned and executed with the utmost discretion, and the team members involved need to be informed of the sensitivity of the information they would become privy to.

For a workforce that has been holding its breath while waiting for the other shoe to drop, the sooner it can be communicated "it's over," the better. In some cases, when the layoff action has been decided on, but for operational reasons it cannot take place until a particular date, it is good to communicate the layoffs to the impacted employees as soon as possible, allowing the time until their last day as additional transition, and reducing the stress levels in the organization. The sooner everyone is informed in an organized manner, the better. The impacted employees get additional time to look for another job. The non-impacted employees can finally breathe easier. Teams can start rebuilding, email addresses and phone numbers are exchanged; the healing begins.

Another critical piece of the layoff communication is an alignment table—allowing the remaining employees to know whom to contact for information on the terminated employees' projects. This apparently minor piece of communication has an indirect benefit, as it reduces dramatically the appetite for hallway speculation and it speaks to strategy and vision. "Yes, we found ourselves in a position to have to reduce our workforce, but we have carefully examined all tasks and undergoing projects, identified those deemed critical to the company's survival, we are going to keep working on them, and this is who will take over."

Severance

Although the financial situation and cash availability might be not so good during a turnaround, if at all possible, we should allow good severance packages for our employees. Here are the main reasons in support of this recommendation:

- Some might be recalled. Having a history of treating them with respect and caring for their well-being will generate a positive atmosphere at the time of the recall and reintegration.

- The company should preserve its positive reputation in the community and in the job market. Once the downturn is over, that will help recruit valuable employees.

Aftermath

When layoffs are finally over, there is a bit of survivor's guilt happening, especially with tenured employees who have lost long-time friends and colleagues. This is quite normal and should be addressed with communication, as leaders reunite their teams and realign their goals.

There is also an effervescence that takes place, an enthusiasm that comes from the relief, and the implicit recognition of one's value, of having been selected to stay with the company. This effervescence, while it might be short lasting, can easily be capitalized on and turned into the fuel of great future performance and team spirit.

Chapter 19
Accurate Revenue Forecasting

Whenever making data-driven decisions regarding cost-cutting actions during a turnaround, there is a pitfall hidden in the numbers: inaccurate revenue forecasting. We'll explore it using the example illustrated in the previous chapter.

EXPL Inc. is ready to close down dealership locations, to ensure its expenses are right-sized to match the sales revenue forecast of $396M for the current year. But—and this is the catch—the more locations it closes, the more revenue it will lose, thus steering away from reaching the $396M sales revenue. The $396M forecast was issued considering a 38-dealership location base. In our study of EXPL's case, the loss of revenue is apparent, easy to spot, and measure, although it poses additional challenges to the turnaround. In most cases though, the loss of revenue is not entirely apparent, leaving many well-meaning decision makers feeling they are chasing an ever-eluding moving target, when, in fact, their actions are pushing the threshold away.

Let's examine the impact of the location closures recommendations on EXPL's revenue forecast. The initial look is in Fig. 19.1, reflecting a sales revenue forecast for the current year of $397.07M annualized, and a negative EBT of $31.56M (head office excluded).

	XPeRank—Revenue and EBT Forecasting				
	Location ID	Monthly Revenue ($M)	Expenses ($M)	EBT ($M)	Recommended Action
*	22	$ 1.77	$ 1.02	$ 0.75	Stays Open
*	23	$ 1.68	$ 1.11	$ 0.57	Stays Open
*	29	$ 1.24	$ 0.67	$ 0.57	Stays Open
*	1	$ 1.13	$ 1.13	$ -	Restructure - Make Profitable
*	2	$ 1.15	$ 1.23	$ (0.08)	Restructure - Make Profitable
*	7	$ 1.08	$ 1.01	$ 0.07	Stays Open
*	31	$ 1.13	$ 1.26	$ (0.13)	Restructure - Make Profitable
	34	$ 0.61	$ 0.46	$ 0.16	Stays Open
	15	$ 0.99	$ 1.00	$ (0.01)	Restructure - Make Profitable
*	10	$ 1.04	$ 1.09	$ (0.05)	Restructure - Make Profitable
*	20	$ 1.11	$ 1.21	$ (0.10)	Restructure - Make Profitable
	14	$ 0.74	$ 0.65	$ 0.09	Stays Open
	3	$ 0.53	$ 0.40	$ 0.13	Stays Open
	8	$ 0.54	$ 0.42	$ 0.12	Stays Open
*	32	$ 1.11	$ 1.24	$ (0.13)	Restructure - Make Profitable
	37	$ 0.65	$ 0.57	$ 0.09	Stays Open
*	11	$ 1.05	$ 1.16	$ (0.11)	Restructure - Make Profitable
*	30	$ 1.06	$ 1.22	$ (0.16)	Restructure - Make Profitable
*	24	$ 1.27	$ 1.77	$ (0.50)	Restructure - Make Profitable
*	35	$ 1.11	$ 1.42	$ (0.31)	Restructure - Make Profitable
	9	$ 0.43	$ 0.31	$ 0.12	Stays Open
*	18	$ 1.12	$ 1.46	$ (0.34)	Restructure - Make Profitable
*	19	$ 1.23	$ 1.82	$ (0.59)	Restructure - Make Profitable
	36	$ 0.36	$ 0.26	$ 0.10	Stays Open
	12	$ 0.38	$ 0.31	$ 0.07	Stays Open
	25	$ 0.43	$ 0.38	$ 0.06	Stays Open
	38	$ 0.45	$ 0.45	$ 0.00	Restructure - Make Profitable
	27	$ 0.85	$ 1.04	$ (0.19)	Close
	13	$ 0.85	$ 1.05	$ (0.20)	Close
	21	$ 0.91	$ 1.22	$ (0.31)	Close
	6	$ 0.47	$ 0.57	$ (0.10)	Close
	17	$ 0.89	$ 1.22	$ (0.33)	Close
	33	***$ 0.76***	***$ 1.02***	***$ (0.26)***	***Restructure - Make Profitable***
	28	$ 0.89	$ 1.29	$ (0.40)	Close
	4	$ 0.38	$ 0.47	$ (0.09)	Close
	16	$ 0.81	$ 1.36	$ (0.55)	Close
	26	$ 0.65	$ 1.02	$ (0.37)	Close
	5	***$ 0.27***	***$ 0.46***	***$ (0.19)***	***Restructure - Make Profitable***
	Total	**$ 33.09**		**$ (2.63)**	
	Annualized ($ M)	**$ 397.07**		**$ (31.56)**	

Fig. 19.1. EXPL locations with revenue, EBT, and recommendations.

Assuming the locations recommended for closure in Phase 1 have been closed, and the locations in need of restructuring are still undergoing their turnaround action, but generating revenue at their normal rates, the adjusted monthly revenue forecast would look like it is shown in Fig. 19.2.

	XPeRank—Revenue and EBT Forecasting				
	Location ID	Monthly Revenue ($M)	Expenses ($M)	EBT ($M)	Recommended Action
*	22	$ 1.77	$ 1.02	$ 0.75	Stays Open
*	23	$ 1.68	$ 1.11	$ 0.57	Stays Open
*	29	$ 1.24	$ 0.67	$ 0.57	Stays Open
*	1	$ 1.12	$ 1.13	$ (0.01)	Restructure - Make Profitable
*	2	$ 1.15	$ 1.23	$ (0.08)	Restructure - Make Profitable
*	7	$ 1.08	$ 1.01	$ 0.07	Stays Open
*	31	$ 1.13	$ 1.26	$ (0.13)	Restructure - Make Profitable
	34	$ 0.61	$ 0.46	$ 0.16	Stays Open
	15	$ 0.99	$ 1.00	$ (0.01)	Restructure - Make Profitable
*	10	$ 1.04	$ 1.09	$ (0.05)	Restructure - Make Profitable
*	20	$ 1.11	$ 1.21	$ (0.10)	Restructure - Make Profitable
	14	$ 0.74	$ 0.65	$ 0.09	Stays Open
	3	$ 0.53	$ 0.40	$ 0.13	Stays Open
	8	$ 0.54	$ 0.42	$ 0.12	Stays Open
*	32	$ 1.11	$ 1.24	$ (0.13)	Restructure - Make Profitable
	37	$ 0.65	$ 0.57	$ 0.09	Stays Open
*	11	$ 1.05	$ 1.16	$ (0.11)	Restructure - Make Profitable
*	30	$ 1.06	$ 1.22	$ (0.16)	Restructure - Make Profitable
*	24	$ 1.27	$ 1.77	$ (0.50)	Restructure - Make Profitable
*	35	$ 1.11	$ 1.42	$ (0.31)	Restructure - Make Profitable
	9	$ 0.43	$ 0.31	$ 0.12	Stays Open
*	18	$ 1.12	$ 1.46	$ (0.34)	Restructure - Make Profitable
*	19	$ 1.23	$ 1.82	$ (0.59)	Restructure - Make Profitable
	36	$ 0.36	$ 0.26	$ 0.10	Stays Open
	12	$ 0.38	$ 0.31	$ 0.07	Stays Open
	25	$ 0.43	$ 0.38	$ 0.06	Stays Open
	38	$ 0.44	$ 0.45	$ (0.00)	Restructure - Make Profitable
	27	$ -	$ -	$ -	Close
	13	$ -	$ -	$ -	Close
	21	$ -	$ -	$ -	Close
	6	$ -	$ -	$ -	Close
	17	$ -	$ -	$ -	Close
	33	***$ 0.76***	***$ 1.02***	***$ (0.26)***	***Restructure - Make Profitable***
	28	$ -	$ -	$ -	Close
	4	$ -	$ -	$ -	Close
	16	$ -	$ -	$ -	Close
	26	$ -	$ -	$ -	Close
	5	***$ 0.27***	***$ 0.46***	***$ (0.19)***	***Restructure - Make Profitable***
	Total	$ 26.38		$ (0.10)	
	Annualized ($ M)	$ 316.54		$ (1.22)	

Fig. 19.2. Impact on revenue and EBT of location closure actions.

The first thing to notice is the drop of $80M in sales revenue. This moves the target further away, as our initial challenge was to become profitable at $396M. Well, we are not yet there. However, the second thing to notice is that our EBT, while still negative, is only $ -1.22M, compared to $ -31.56M. We're still losing money, but at a slower rate. This means we are making progress, taking steps in the right direction. Can we fix the problem? We must ! Possible solutions are to increase revenue, make further cut costs, or both.

In our example, we have proposed the formation of an online sales division, based at the head office. That will add revenue (forecast based on competitive benchmarking analysis), and add limited cost. Let's add it in Fig. 19.3.

	XPeRank—Revenue and EBT Forecasting				
	Location ID	Monthly Revenue ($M)	Expenses ($M)	EBT ($M)	Recommended Action
*	22	$ 1.77	$ 1.02	$ 0.75	Stays Open
*	23	$ 1.68	$ 1.11	$ 0.57	Stays Open
*	29	$ 1.24	$ 0.67	$ 0.57	Stays Open
*	1	$ 1.12	$ 1.13	$ (0.01)	Restructure - Make Profitable
*	2	$ 1.15	$ 1.23	$ (0.08)	Restructure - Make Profitable
*	7	$ 1.08	$ 1.01	$ 0.07	Stays Open
*	31	$ 1.13	$ 1.26	$ (0.13)	Restructure - Make Profitable
	34	$ 0.61	$ 0.46	$ 0.16	Stays Open
	15	$ 0.99	$ 1.00	$ (0.01)	Restructure - Make Profitable
*	10	$ 1.04	$ 1.09	$ (0.05)	Restructure - Make Profitable
*	20	$ 1.11	$ 1.21	$ (0.10)	Restructure - Make Profitable
	14	$ 0.74	$ 0.65	$ 0.09	Stays Open
	3	$ 0.53	$ 0.40	$ 0.13	Stays Open
	8	$ 0.54	$ 0.42	$ 0.12	Stays Open
*	32	$ 1.11	$ 1.24	$ (0.13)	Restructure - Make Profitable
	37	$ 0.65	$ 0.57	$ 0.09	Stays Open
*	11	$ 1.05	$ 1.16	$ (0.11)	Restructure - Make Profitable
*	30	$ 1.06	$ 1.22	$ (0.16)	Restructure - Make Profitable
*	24	$ 1.27	$ 1.77	$ (0.50)	Restructure - Make Profitable
*	35	$ 1.11	$ 1.42	$ (0.31)	Restructure - Make Profitable
	9	$ 0.43	$ 0.31	$ 0.12	Stays Open
*	18	$ 1.12	$ 1.46	$ (0.34)	Restructure - Make Profitable
*	19	$ 1.23	$ 1.82	$ (0.59)	Restructure - Make Profitable
	36	$ 0.36	$ 0.26	$ 0.10	Stays Open
	12	$ 0.38	$ 0.31	$ 0.07	Stays Open
	25	$ 0.43	$ 0.38	$ 0.06	Stays Open
	38	$ 0.44	$ 0.45	$ (0.00)	Restructure - Make Profitable
	33	***$ 0.76***	***$ 1.02***	***$ (0.26)***	***Restructure - Make Profitable***
	5	***$ 0.27***	***$ 0.46***	***$ (0.19)***	***Restructure - Make Profitable***
	Online sales Unit	***$ 6.21***	***$ 4.54***	***$ 1.67***	***Create New Unit***
	Total	**$ 32.59**		**$ 1.57**	
	Annualized ($ M)	**$ 391.06**		**$ 18.82**	

Fig. 19.3. Impact on revenue and EBT of location closure actions and new online sales unit.

The new online sales unit will almost compensate us almost back to the $396M plan, and put us in positive EBT land. We're still off target through, but minimally. Further actions are required, in addition to a continuous improvement strategy.

We'll cover more about this in Chapter 31.
This was a clear-cut example of "moving target" sales revenue forecast. In the reality of complex operations, the diminishing sales effect of various operational turnaround and cost-reduction actions is quite elusive. Here are a few reasons why, with examples:

The action influences sales indirectly, through customer referrals and brand image. For many companies it is impossible to quantify the impact of referrals to their overall sales volume, or how many points of decreased brand popularity makes $1M in lost sales. Therefore, some cost-cutting actions that would seem to make dollar-sense at first sight must be examined through a customer-centric mindset. Examples of such cost-cutting actions with serious negative customer impact are:

- Outsourcing customer-facing roles to offshore locations, thus adding cultural barriers, language barriers, security concerns, and potential bias on the path of customer satisfaction. Outsourcing these roles offshore has already started to demonstrate its disadvantages, and we are seeing large corporations revisiting the idea and bringing the contact and support centers back to North America.
- Sacrificing quality in the interest of cost. Once a product's reputation has gone bad, it is costly to recover and regain the lost terrain. Customers will perceive drops in product or service quality while maintaining the price as an attempt to take advantage of their trust and loyalty, and they will take their business elsewhere.

Taking actions without knowing or considering the customers' deterrents to purchase. If our customers hesitate to purchase our products due to our warranty coverage, currently below the industry average, further reducing that warranty policy span will generate losses in revenue, although quite complicated to quantify and forecast without in-depth studies.

Not having quantified or understood the impact of various marketing channels. Cutting media spending in an area will lead to some loss in sales. Do we understand the mechanisms behind it? Do we know how to compensate? Marketing spend should be reviewed periodically through the filter of return on investment (ROI), and prioritized by channel, region, or targeted audience based on efficiency and impact on sales.

Failing to consider the growing impact of the social media, the damage it can do in the hands of unhappy customers, and the potential it can represent in the hands of happy customers. Our world, as we knew it, has changed. Online social media is a powerful sales-driving force, which can work both ways. Quantifying the potential dollar impact—positive or negative—of a high-visibility consumer posting remains a challenge. However, steering online media in the right direction—to help promote rather than detract—can do no harm.

With all this in mind, we cannot be too cautious when stating a sales revenue forecast, especially if we are in the midst of numerous process improvement, cost-cutting, and restructuring changes. Therefore, sales revenue forecast should be an on-going exercise, revisited after each change is implemented, allowing the turnaround action plan to be aligned with the revised values.

Chapter 20
Variable versus Fixed in Volatile Sales Environments

If the demand for our product or service is fluctuating—and this is what most companies see during challenging economic times—and it cannot be rigorously planned, the need for a highly variable operational structure is increased. More specifically, the less we can count on our sales levels, the more we need to keep our operational cost structure variable, so we can manage costs effectively while walking on the moving sands of unsteady demand.

Many vertically integrated companies seem to come to a crossroad when demand drops below a certain threshold or becomes highly unstable. In most cases, these organizations have an intricate internal supply chain, developed while vertical integration became their preferred method of control. Especially in complex manufacturing operations, this translates into a large fixed asset and cost base, with limited cost variability in times of volatile demand.

Such structures are highly preferred during peak economic times, when companies see constant growth and want to maintain a good grip on the quality of their products, control cost, and implement just-in-time strategies. However, once demand drops, little can be done overnight in such a case to drop costs significantly and keep up with lower demand levels, thus maintaining profitability. No matter how keen everyone is on finding every possible cost-cutting opportunity and every process efficiency, if a plant has no demand, it produces no value—just quickly burns through significant resources. Therefore, assessing the entire

supply chain structure from a unit efficiency and competitive advantage perspective becomes the key to profitability.
There is a way to manage through this challenge without significantly sacrificing any of our vertical integration benefits: quality, cost, and just-in-time (JIT) strategies. For each component of our supply chain, we have to ask ourselves: do we have a competitive advantage there? If yes, let's keep it in-house and find ways in which we can increase the cost variability of the processes involved. If no, let's identify those suppliers who do have the competitive advantage, and buy what we need from them, with rigorous quality, cost, and inventory controls in place.

Case Study

Using an example, we will work the high-level view of such an exercise. Our example is, this time, a mineral water bottling and distribution company, in need of dropping some ballast to achieve maneuverability. The company has a definite and obvious competitive advantage in its water sources—identified and under concession with the respective governments for extended periods of time.

The water-testing lab—currently in-house—is probably less cost-effective than other labs; however, it is a relatively small operation and all the equipment has already been purchased and paid for. Furthermore, the results are available quickly due to its close proximity to the water batches; so we will keep the lab in-house. The decision should be revisited at a future time when equipment will become obsolete, or in need of replacement.
The bottle-manufacturing unit—a dinosaur still clinging to life—is from back in the days when having a customized bottle would cost a fortune. The competitive advantage in manufacturing bottles has long since been lost; producing the bottles in-house generates $0.07 per unit in additional cost versus buying the bottles from a high-volume manufacturer—shipping to our bottling facility included. The decisions are as follows:

- Source the best bottle suppliers and negotiate tiered volume discounts, stringent quality standards, and JIT strategy.
- Examine the current design, look, and feel of the bottles and discuss with the new manufacturer if minor adjustments are indicated, in order to reduce costs and bring the bottles into the 21st century. After all, the bottle design, specs, and materials formulation have not been refreshed since 1974.

These potential changes will have to keep the brand image in mind and not cause consumer confusion.

- Once the bottle supplier is in place, dismantle and liquidate the existing bottle-manufacturing unit. Retain, cross-train, and reassign the highly skilled workforce, if applicable.

The water-bottling line is a close call; we seem to have limited competitive advantage in the bottling business, therefore we will keep the line as an in-house operation, for strategic purposes and good quality control. We do, however, need to increase variability in the unit; therefore the line is in need of future evaluation from this perspective. Because we have some competitive advantage in this business, we might even consider offering bottling services to the wine industry, to further leverage existing capacities, which would be freed by a more variable process design. Furthermore, we might explore other products that would leverage these capacities—potentially entering the wine import, wholesale, and distribution business.

Packaging will stay in-house, due to proximity and feasibility. However, the antiquated, resource-hungry, heavy packaging is in need of redesign, with a refreshed look and modern materials. The cardboard box manufacturing line needs to go away. Sourcing packaging materials will bring the opportunity of some packaging redesign and cost optimization conversations, with experts in packaging invited to provide quotes. The same stringent quality controls, JIT, and tiered cost need to happen.

The phone order-entry and service unit is a surprise. We have a definite competitive advantage over any North-American based call-center, outsourcing facility, as we come in at 10 percent lower cost per agent-hour than the market rate. Offshore outsourcing does come in at 12 percent lower than our costs per logged agent hour. However, with offshore we have the clear risk of inflated call duration, increased order error rates, and aggravating our standing business clients through language barriers. Furthermore, in the 50-some years the company has been in business, most of its business clients who call to place orders are years-long relationships, on first-name basis with our staff. This loyalty and familiarity are worth far more than the doubtful 12 percent cost reduction offshore would bring. The service and order-entry center stays put.

This exercise into finding variability opportunities and working toward achieving a lean, flexible supply chain needs to happen periodically. New technologies surface every year, new materials, ideas, and equipment. They are worth exploring and measuring against. That will ensure not only a successful turnaround now, when it is needed, but also readiness for smooth sailing through troubled waters in the future.

Chapter 21
Note on Decision Making

Turnarounds bring with them a flurry of decisions of all sorts: big and small, tough and easy, long-term and short-term impact. These decisions need to have undisputable value; they need to be good decisions, made fast, by the right people. A formalized decision-making process will ensure we are successful in achieving this goal. Having some rigor around the decision process will bring significant benefits:

- Decisions will be data and process driven.
- Decisions will be made by the correct decision maker(s), and with inputs from all relevant stakeholders.
- Decisions will be consistent in nature throughout the organization, allowing comparisons between decisions, learning from bad decisions and good decisions equally.
- All parties involved will be more likely to think outside the box.
- Decisions will be made faster and be met with less resistance.
- There will be no circling back on decisions, second thoughts, and reevaluations, if no significant new information is available.
- There will be no personal agendas steering the decisions to support the interest of one person.
- There will be more courage and accountability around decisions.

This is not a rigor to be applied for all decisions; it would become time consuming to the point that it would freeze all resources involved and paralyze the business. This type of rigor should apply to strategic, complex decisions, where the right decision is not obvious and the stakes are high. For such situations, following these steps will ensure the fast, consistent delivery of good decisions:

1. Formulate a problem statement. What are we trying to solve? Old wisdom says "The answer is hidden in the question itself," so we will apply this principle and formulate a short, to-the-point problem statement: what are we trying to achieve?

2. Identify who the decision maker(s) should be. The fewer, the merrier. Empower them and hold them accountable. Identify who should contribute with data and/or ideas to the decision-making process, and who are the stakeholders who need to be involved. This is the decision-making team.

3. Gather and structure all relevant data regarding the decision; financial implications, historic data, benchmarking data, etc. Explore choices creatively, look beyond the normal, the routine, the "what's been done before." Think outside the box, and reward creative thinkers who bring revolutionary approaches. Identify all needed data and make it available. Analyze the data and draw conclusions. Make sure the data is accurate, so the conclusions can be a true reflection of the reality.

4. Explore the available options, based on the data analysis. Evaluate the options and select those that make the most sense in helping achieve the things we want faster, more affordably, and more effectively.

5. Ensure proper execution on the decision; otherwise, even the best of the decisions are worthless. Communicate to all parties involved the decision that was reached and on what basis. This will ensure alignment and buy-in, with less challenge. Plan the implementation immediately and with key controls in place, to measure the effectiveness and the result of the decision. Drive learning from these results, whether good or bad.

Let's demonstrate how this rigor can be applied, through an example, and see how the theory meets the practical realities of business.

Case Study

In this example, a fashion apparel company is undergoing a dramatic turnaround action, where all costs, departmental spending and budgets need to be cut by at least 20 percent to ensure the company's survival. Faced with a 20 percent budget challenge, the manufacturing department has some tough decisions to make; but which are the right ones?

Background: The company is an established apparel manufacturer, owner of numerous popular brands of leisure garments. It has manufacturing facilities onshore and offshore—Vietnam and China—all company owned. North American textile and apparel manufacturing has seen a consistent decline during the recent years, pushing more and more of the company's production volume toward the offshore capacities.

Step 1: Problem statement. "Apparel manufacturing needs to cut spending by 20 percent as soon as possible, while maintaining or improving the quality of the finished product."

Step 2: This decision belongs with the head of manufacturing. Key stakeholders in this case would be the plant managers, the logistics leader, the quality assurance leader, an IT representative, and cross-functional representation as needed—Finance, Human Resources.

Step 3: A quick look at the production and labor data, both onshore and offshore, shows workforce occupancy is quite high, therefore cutting labor hours by 20 percent would lead to lower quality and drops in output. Brainstorming ideas from the team:

- Closing the company-owned manufacturing facilities and outsourcing the production—offshore, with rates, conditions, and terms—aka entering the cut-make-trim (CMT) market as a client.
- Explore other, more affordable locations for the company-owned offshore plants, in new emerging markets (that is, the African Growth and Opportunity Act—AGOA).
- Increasing occupancy and optimization of process flows via computerized workflow optimization—resulting in potential labor cost reduction.
- Reducing the labor hours in the plants—currently operating in three shifts, and switching them to two-shift operations, thus reducing labor costs associated with a night shift.

- Closing the onshore facilities and moving the load offshore—the design group, pattern development, sample development, and testing lab.

Step 4: Based on the ideas and subsequent data analysis, here are the findings and decisions:

- Computerized workflow optimization, combined with cutting automation at the offshore plants will generate a net 7.8 percent of the needed 20 percent reduction in operating costs. Out of the 7.8 percent, almost half (3.4 percentage points) comes from textile cost savings due to cutting automation and automated pattern layout.
- Switching the plants to two-shift operations will create spare capacities in the night shift—both real estate and equipment. However, chasing potential lessees for the space and equipment will probably not yield the expected results in time. A better choice is to use part of the capacity to absorb some of the onshore production, while for the rest of the available capacity, entering the market as a CMT vendor seems like a better idea, because the company has a proven competitive advantage in apparel manufacturing. Furthermore, due to its North American headquarters, the company can secure CMT clients on American soil, with higher profitability. This alternative comes with elasticity—the company is well set for future growth, ready to expand its own label capacity by almost 30 percent without further investment. Cutting the third shift at all plants generates another 6.2 percent of savings without any negative impact on output or quality.
- Moving the cotton-based manufacturing from onshore to offshore manufacturing and alternate sourcing the cotton fabrics will generate another 2.7 percent of the needed operating cost reduction. Finally, securing CMT business for only 25 percent of the newly created capacities will bring enough revenue to compensate the 3.3 percent cost savings left to find.
- The high-end labels will continue to be manufactured onshore; the labs and new product development facilities will also remain onshore. All data suggests no net gain whatsoever from moving them offshore; quite the opposite, as new product development benefits by the cultural presence in the targeted market.

Step 5: Communication and execution. Properly communicate to the organization what decisions have been made, the basis for reaching them, and the key milestones in implementing them. Special attention needs to be given to managing the reductions in workforce in the plants, and the market's perception of the change. Owners are assigned for all steps involved in the execution of the decision. This exercise is now complete.

Two things are notable with any decision-making process:

1. A corporation is not a democracy. Not all employees need to vote or agree on who the next sheet metal supplier should be. Decision makers should be encouraged to decide what makes the best sense for the business, not to try to make everyone happy, or cave under peer pressure.

2. At the next level of escalation, send away all complaints regarding the formal decisions already made. Stand behind your decision makers, as their empowerment and your support is what will make them be brave, bold, accountable, creative, and successful.

This example illustrates the broad spectrum of ideas and potential fixes covered by the formalized decision-making process, and how the process stimulates out-of-the-box thinking and courageous approaches to challenges. This type of decision-making process will greatly contribute to the long-term success and stability of any turnaround action.

Chapter 22
Focus on Quality

Cutting costs at the expense of quality is a bad idea. It backfires in many ways, some quantifiable, some not. Often enough though, the first place everyone goes for immediate cost-cutting initiatives is not toward process optimization and restructuring, but toward removing cost from the actual product. Product—as in the quality of materials, manufacturing, quality control, kid glove service, in short, everything that made our product special and our customers loyal. This method—cutting cost at all cost—is usually bringing a higher price tag than the actual savings it generates.

In recent years, we have all seen it happen. The quality standards we were used to 20 years ago are simply no longer available, no matter how hard we look and—in most cases—how much we are willing to pay. Everything in the stores is now mostly in China, and the alternate offer seems to have vanished from the shelves. Every now and then a massive recall, or huge scandal, reminds us how widely spread this issue has become. Therefore, staying competitive in such a market is, in almost all cases, not a quality-driven strategy, but a cost-driven one.

Therefore, the challenge is maintaining the highest quality possible while lowering costs and staying competitive in a cost-driven market. How do we do that? By keeping in mind the following points:

Evaluate a Net Return on Cost Reduction by Factoring in Warranty

It is easy to jump to conclusions that illustrate significant savings if we reduce the thickness of the housing material for our new line of HDTVs. This is easy math. What is not so easy is to factor in the potential increases in warranty rates and post-warranty defects. The first will generate cost through the warranty claims. The second will generate brand image deterioration, and losses in consumer confidence and referral, therefore, negatively impacting future sales of all our models. In some unfortunate cases, the third unwanted set of consequences can appear—recalls due to potential hazardous malfunctions, or legal liability over some losses of property and/or life. So if we saved $1.50 by cutting on the housing material but we increase the warranty claims by as little as 2 percentage points, the result of this action is net negative just from the cost of servicing the warranty policy.

It is, however, hard to resist the temptation of jumping on the first quick fix in terms of cutting materials and manufacturing quality. Sometimes, leadership is also at fault, by pushing people to find unreasonably large cost savings fast, without due process, and by discouraging any carefully balanced approach or pushback. Leaders, presented with the huge opportunity that looks too good to be true, should assume it probably is. They should ask the teams "Have you considered all implications, both short and long term? How will this affect the quality, safety, and reliability of our product? How will this impact our customers' satisfaction with our product?" If the answers to these questions are not positive and supported by data, they should encourage the teams to take a step back and find other opportunities, where the net return would stay positive.

Have Stringent Quality Stipulations in any Supplier Contract

All suppliers should be held to strict standards for quality. The contracts should stipulate in detail what acceptable quality is, and a provision for lower quality that exceeds a set percentage of the total. Any supplier should be able to guarantee and maintain quality standards, with requirements and key measures stipulated and tolerances indicated. The contract should also indicate clearly who will absorb the cost of low-quality products, how quality control will happen, and what the process would be for returning defective products. The more challenging the economic environment is, the more the suppliers will also try to cut their costs. Only this time you are the customer. Therefore, a safe approach is to have rigorous testing done and second-tier suppliers lined up.

More on this in Chapter 23, which is dedicated to sourcing, contract

rigor, and finding the right suppliers.

Improve Processes, Innovate, Refresh Materials and Technology, Rather Than Cut Costs without Discerning

Turnarounds are not the best times to think investments and new technology. But . . . What if the new technology would have a positive ROI within three months? What if the new equipment would bring efficiencies to our processes allowing us to maintain quality yet cut the cost? Sometimes the solutions will be in the process-improvement opportunities, rather than the indiscriminate cost-cutting initiatives.

Most companies, on their path of growth from small to medium to large, patch up processes, rather than rethinking the whole from the ground up. While this could be acceptable for a while, this patching method will incorporate significant inefficiencies along the way. Even if these are noticed at some point, since the company is growing, doing great, and everyone has a lot of money in their budgets, and these inefficiencies almost never are addressed. When on a downturn, it becomes harder to address them, due to time and financial constraints, but it is still better than sacrificing quality instead.

Being a modern, customer-centric organization requires systematic effort along the lines of technology, system and process optimization, and innovation, refreshing them periodically, regardless of the financial state of the business. An example comes to mind—maintenance contracts signed 20 years ago and automatically renewed every year for a laser printer, end up costing more per year than an equivalent new printer. This is how it became more expensive to pay for maintenance than to buy a new printer every year, and repair it under warranty if it breaks. A technology-refreshing fix does not get any easier than this.

The immediate prize of the turnaround is survival; however, in any turnaround plan we need to consider post-turnaround stabilization and future growth. This is why we need to maintain the focus on quality. Quality will make customers loyal, will ensure a good reputation, and contribute to market-share growth. In short, quality-focused turnaround strategies are optimal for customer-centric environments.

Chapter 23
Notes on Strategic Sourcing

Sourcing is an art. Quite like any other form of art, sourcing requires dedication, creativity, a contextual, three-dimensional vision, and a lot of passion. An artist's work is never done; neither is sourcing.

Strategic sourcing has changed in the past decades, as the economies are now of global reach and highly dynamic. A vendor relationship used to be a life-long, personal relationship back in the 1950s, 1960s, up to the 1990s—when everything abruptly changed. New concepts, such as outsourcing, globalization, and emerging markets, invaded the sourcing world and forever altered its mechanisms.

In this day's dynamic, global market, we need to turn sourcing into an advantage, especially for the financially troubled company undergoing a turnaround. A few key points are worthy of note:

Quality

Especially in adverse economic environments, but most likely everywhere in the world and at any time, companies are cutting costs with little or no respect for quality. Your providers are, most likely, among them. The challenge is to make sure the quality standards remain high, as per your initial assessment of the vendor's capabilities. Having the supplier locked into a contract with detailed quality stipulations, quality control mechanisms, clearly defined acceptable defect rates, well-documented key measures and tolerances, and penalties for poor quality, is probably the safest way to protect the end quality of our product. After all, our product is just as good as the sum of all the defects of all its components and its labor.

Negotiate Terms When You Don't Need Them

Just like credit, supplier-payment terms are easier to negotiate when the supplier is eager to get your signature on the contract and a new client secured. Leaving terms to whatever was stipulated on the template contract form could prove an expensive oversight, especially in the eventuality that cash should become scarce and difficult to manage. However, having terms pushed to the limit of the vendor's availability leaves little or no room for renegotiating terms later; therefore supplier payments need to be maintained on schedule, and cash flow managed carefully.

Have Alternate Providers Lined Up

Applying the centuries-old wisdom of not putting all your eggs in a single basket, it would be smart to have more than one vendor for a critical product or service in your supply chain, whenever possible. This flexibility, although it does add to the hassle of vendor and quality management, brings significant benefits:

- **Being able to shift loads and compensate swiftly for the loss of a vendor**, with no delay. In the case of a vendor going bankrupt or breaching contractual terms, having an alternate already lined up and loaded with a percentage of our needs makes quick response possible in such contingencies. Understanding each vendor's available and stretch capacities can be helpful when faced with abrupt changes, or the unexpected.
- **Stable supply in the face of natural disaster disruptions**—whether snowstorms, floods, or earthquakes—they don't hit everywhere at the same time. Business continuity and timely deliveries are critical for just-in-time processes; this method provides added security.
- **Having vendors in an on-going competitive stance**—from all perspectives. Cost, product, materials quality, terms, speed of delivery, quality of client service—the competing vendors will be maintained in check from all these perspectives.
- **Stable supply in the face of our own cash flow issues**—should we become unable to make payments on time to one

or more vendors, or should we max out our credit limit with a specific vendor, it would be beneficial to have an alternate vendor already identified and ready to take over the entire capacity. Sometimes vendors tighten their credit limits and terms for clients with known financial difficulties, as an added precaution. Not being the only vendor will also force them to remain competitive from this perspective.

Renegotiate Contracts Every Year

We are constantly striving to improve our products and services; innovate, discover, and implement revolutionary materials, technologies and systems; and increase our efficiencies. So does everyone else—or almost. This alone is the first good reason to repeat our sourcing exercise every year and discover what else has become available. Although it might seem strenuous and costly, this exercise ensures we are keeping up with trends, quality standards, materials, processes, delivery times, and—why not—our competition and our customers.

Second is another good reason—offsetting at least a part of the price tag of this repeated exercise, is the cost savings we might discover. We have recently become more competitive with our product offering, but we're not the only ones. Therefore, it might be worth looking into.

Third, and most surprising, in some cases we might discover we have a competitive advantage in an area or a market we had no idea about, hence opening the door to picking up additional business from this newly discovered market, thus further leveraging our existing capacities.

Go Global Wisely

Wherever applicable, global is the keyword for every thorough sourcing exercise. While there are areas where local will forever stay local—as in trash removal, for example—for mostly everything else there are global markets eager to sign up our business.

There is huge controversy on the issue of globalization and this is not the place to reiterate the main pros and cons of it. The only thing worth mentioning in this context is long-term vision. No one intentionally ends up being penny-smart and dollar-foolish, but it's known to have happened more than a few times with global sourcing.

What do most bad global sourcing decisions have in common? Lack of long-term vision, doubled by haste to find immediate, yet significant savings. All these bad deals started with an offer too good to be true, and someone preoccupied with only today's results. Usually, an offer too good to be true usually is, and ignored hidden costs will surface without delay, together with potential drops in quality.

If getting a new supplier offshore set up and ready to go was a challenge, bringing it back to North America is an even bigger one. Therefore, with careful attention and great consideration given to where the long-term strategy should lead us, we should explore what emerging and established markets are ready to offer us. This is how we will find the edge needed to help us turnaround and stabilize in a cost-effective way.

Look—And Analyze—Before You Leap

From this perspective, there are multiple facets to consider carefully before deciding on a new vendor, especially an offshore one:
Any calculation of potential savings brought by outsourcing a particular process usually fails to recognize early-on significant losses of efficiency. The calls handled by the outsourced call center take more time, due to cultural and language barriers. The lead generation calls will have a lower success rate than the in-house team's calls. The quality of the waterproof hospital scrubs will suffer at the mercy of failures in the static-free environment needed in the packing area, spiking the defect rates to unprecedented values, by causing sterile accessories to become, in fact, non-sterile.

The application developed offshore will have numerous bugs that should have been caught during the first user-testing phase, but are still manifesting despite all commitments for immediate containment. The "contains no peanuts" statement on our chocolate label is not accurate anymore, because a competitor with a peanut-based formulation is using the third shift at the same manufacturing location, and is tainting our manufacturing environment. And so on. All these are trade-offs for the savings and variability we are hoping to achieve by buying instead of making.

While it is common knowledge these tradeoffs exist more or less in any such deal, failing to quantify them correctly in both size and impact could prove to be a costly decision. Some of these tradeoffs are solely impacting the bottom line; others impact our customers' decision to buy, or our brand reputation.

Therefore, we should complete a careful and thorough analysis on any such potential tradeoffs, to ensure qualified decisions are being made, and net benefits are quantified correctly. As an added precaution, wherever possible, perform test runs with new vendors before switching off our internal capacities or existing vendors.

With the above points considered, sourcing is one of the elements most likely to make or break our competitive advantage, our brand reputation, and our customers' loyalty. Therefore, strategic sourcing done right is integral to any successful turnaround.

Chapter 24
The Right Metrics

Any performance-driven organization is in need of establishing relevant metrics so it can set targets and measure success. These metrics have to be clearly defined and documented, to avoid confusion and errors in reporting. Each department or business unit can select and define relevant metrics, which can be rolled up to reflect the few key measures of profitability, quality, efficiency, output, etc., which reflect the health of a business. In this chapter and the following two, we will explore a data-matrix approach to metrics, goals and objectives, and performance appraisals.

A Balanced Approach

The selection of key metrics for a business unit has to be able to provide a 360-degree view of the respective unit: efficiency, quality, effectiveness, and customer centricity. The approach on metrics—hence on performance—should be balanced, therefore ensuring steady, concerted effort, and achievement. This type of stability ensures the success of implementing long-term strategies and vision, rather than short-term, burst-like focus: this month we're all about productivity, next month we're focused on quality, etc.

What constitutes a balanced approach to a business unit's metrics can obviously change from unit to unit, as it is dictated by the specifics of the business. For example, for one department it might be relevant to measure learning and development as a tier-one metric, while for another it is more important to measure output units per hour instead.

Rate Measurements

Most metrics paint a more accurate picture if they are expressed as rates, thus measuring one quantity with respect to another measured quantity. For example, the overall cost to run a business unit for a month can tell us precisely how much money would leave the bank accounts at the end of the month, but gives us no idea of how efficient the department has been operating. To capture the efficiency, a rate measure, a "dollars per unit" type of metric is needed, measuring spend with respect to the plant's output. In this particular example, both measures are needed to paint a wholesome picture. In most cases, through, either one or the other would do; the decision in favor of either being based on whichever brings a more accurate view of what is going on.

The quick self-check set of questions regarding the selection of metrics and targets could sound like this, "If this metric falls below target, will it paint an accurate picture and will it generate response actions? If the business unit is performing substandard, will this metric and its current target level reflect the poor performance?"

Documentation

Once we decide how to measure our business, the next step is to document it for future reference. In complex environments, carefully selected metrics are defined with great accuracy, excluding special causes and exceptions that could lead to either false-negative or false-positive reads.

As an example, for an IT environment it makes great sense to measure a service level defined as "the percentage of service tickets closed under 24 hours." Failure to exclude the cases of remote workers and laptops of traveling executives would cause the service level to show worse on paper than in reality. Deciding to measure "business hours" would cause the target of 24 hours = one day to become 24 hours = three days, therefore painting a rosier picture than before. As departmental leaders and employees come and go, the definitions of metrics tend to fade and lose specificity, as with any form of folklore.

Documenting departmental metrics is not a huge task. It can look like this:

Department Name: Order Entry		Revised Date: 15 Jan
Metric	**Unit of Measurement**	**Definition**
Total Spend	$	The total cost of running the business unit. Includes all payroll, amortization, licenses, and G&A
Cost Per Order	$	Total spend (as above) divided by total orders placed, from all channels except online orders
Conversion Rate	units per contact	The total units ordered divided by total inbound contacts, from all channels except online orders
Labor Efficiency	units per paid labor hour	Total units ordered through all inbound channels except online orders, divided by total logged labor hours
Missing & Wrong	percentage of M&W out of total orders	Total M&W claims divided by total orders - all channels except online orders. Expressed as a percentage

Fig. 24.1. Metrics documentation sheet.

Defining Success

At the time of a turnaround and at any time in the life of a business, success has to be clearly defined, so it can be translated into goals, complete with targets and the right metrics to measure them by. A good question to be answered is, "How do we recognize success when we get there?" If success is not accurately defined, it will end up becoming an ever-moving target, causing misalignment, failure, and frustration at all levels. Here's why.

Success can represent for a $50M-a-year company reaching the $100M threshold. But once the company is achieving sales of $95M a year, reaching $100M doesn't seem like such a big deal; therefore new targets are set with little or no recognition for the current achievements. With an ever-changing frame of reference, recognizing success becomes a forgotten item on the to-do list, lost in the fervor to achieve more and more.

Stopping for a second and reminding everyone where they used to be and where they are today makes for a great introduction into setting new targets and gaining company-wide support and engagement to reach them. It also allows for the "stop and think" milestone to exist, the time where recent achievement can be given some thought to determine what worked and what didn't. It also makes a great time to pay out bonuses or keep our word on the things we promised when being a $100M company seemed like a distant dream.

Especially with turnarounds, success has to be accurately defined, as the goal of the turnaround action: What do we want to achieve from the turnaround plan? What are the deliverables? When do we stop and say, for example, "This was a successful turnaround and it was completed in five-and-a-half months?"

Historic and Perspective Views

With all the metrics already established, defined, and documented, and with the answers on what the deliverables of the turnaround plan should be, we can proceed in laying out the roadmap to success, post-turnaround stabilization, and return to growth. Like everything else, these steps are measurable in the form of targets for our business units.

For example, one of the goals of the turnaround could be turning the currently negative EBT into a positive number—stop the losing money trend. A goal for the post-turnaround stabilization could well be to have consistent, above-zero EBT during a period of six months—aka stabilization—ideally with an upward trend. Finally, the goal for the return to growth phase is to have EBT on an upward trend, with a plan to reach $75M before the end of next year.

This approach allows us to pinpoint goals and target values for all critical metrics in the organization. With this figured out, we could proceed to ensure we are aligned and engaged in our goals, we measure performance consistently, and we recognize and reward achievement fairly.

Chapter 25
Goals and Objectives—Setting and Alignment

This chapter does not bring yet another description about what goals should or should not be; there is sufficient good material available elsewhere. The innovative method we will explore next, named XPeGoals (for Expedient Goals), is a matrixed system designed to ensure success in two of the most challenging areas in goal setting and performance measuring.

The first of the two challenges is obtaining perfect alignment of goals and trickle-down throughout the organization. Second is the delivery of aligned goals, the development of tactical plans, and the achievement of buy-in from the teams, in minimal time—thus avoiding the excruciating meeting-after-meeting drill we all know so well.

This is quite a complex tool, so the best way to present its functionality and application is by the use of an example. The company, in the following case study, is a beauty and health products company, finding itself in need of a turnaround.

Case Study

Company overview: Example Inc. is a wholesale and retail distributor of a variety of health and beauty products, in addition to some nutrition supplements and cosmetic accessories. The company sells through multiple channels:

- Retail—through company-owned stores

- Online shopping—e-commerce
- Authorized distributors—spas and health facilities, grocery stores, convenience stores, etc.

Due to the economic environment, Example Inc. has recently experienced significant losses and is now preparing a dramatic turnaround action, aimed at restoring profitability and market share. In times like these, there is little room for error; the need for alignment on goals and objectives throughout the organization is of the utmost importance, and there is limited time to allow successful alignment through the traditional methods: repeated meetings at team level, followed by one-on-one meetings with each employee, etc.

In terms of organizational structure, this is what our company looks like:

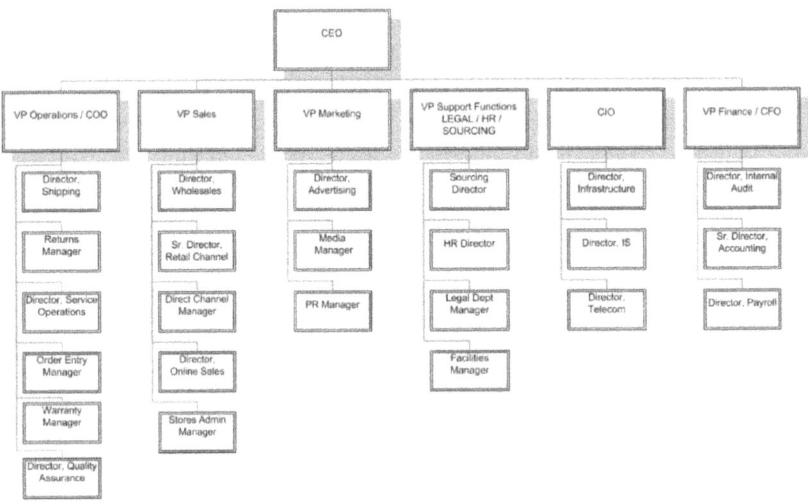

Fig. 25.1. Example Inc. organizational chart.

Methodology—XPeGoals

Step 1: Defining company level strategic goals.

We start building the XPeGoals matrix by defining what are the main strategic goals for Example Inc. Think CEO level—what does the CEO need to achieve in the immediate future? As it is turnaround time for this customer-centric organization, these may well be:

- Positive EBT
- Positive cash flow
- Increase market share
- Now that we're in agreement with what these are, we need to set targets and deadlines for them:
- Positive EBT—reach $5M in three months (by the end of Q1).
- Positive free-cash flow—reach $15M in three months (by the end of Q1).
- Increase market share—recover the past year's loss in market share, reach last January's level of 8.9 percent in three months.

Step 2: Creating the master XPeGoals matrix, with CEO level goals.

Simply put, we create a spreadsheet in which we organize the information above: goals for the first quarter (Q1), scope, KPIs (metrics), and targets. This first view is the CEO-level view—it looks like this:

XPeGoals Example Inc. CEO Level			KPI and Targets Deadline: end of Q1
Goal **What?**		**Scope** **How?**	**Target**
Positive EBT	→		reach $5M EBT
(Earnings Before Tax)	→		
	→		
	→		
	→		
	→		
Positive cash flow	→		reach $15M positive cash flow
	→		
	→		
	→		
Increase market share	→		increase market share by 1 percentage point - to 8.9%
	→		
	→		

Fig. 25.2. Master XPeGoals matrix—initial key organizational goals and objectives setting, with KPIs and deadlines—CEO level.

All the business units will contribute to at least one of these goals. In order to start working on the development of tactical plans and cross-functional alignment, we need to enhance this view a little, by adding stretch targets, bonus levels, and the key alignment indexes.

Step 3: Introducing stretch targets and maximum bonus levels.

We have added stretch target levels and corresponding bonus levels—and it should look like this:

XPeGoals Example Inc. CEO Level			KPI and Targets Deadline: end of Q1		
Goal What?		Scope How?	Target	Stretch Target	Max Bonus Level
Positive EBT (Earnings Before Tax)	→ → → → → →		reach $5M EBT	$5.5M	125%
Positive cash flow	→ → → →		reach $15M positive cash flow	$16.5M	125%
Increase market share	→ → →		increase market share by 1 percentage point - to 8.9%	9.00%	125%

Fig. 25.3. Introducing stretch targets and maximum bonus levels.

The easy way to interpret the stretch target levels and bonus levels is:

- If we achieve the stated goal of $5M EBT, the bonus level corresponding to that is 100 percent.
- If we achieve the stretch goal of $5.5M EBT, then the corresponding bonus level will be 125 percent. Therefore, for 10 percent overachievement in goals, our example company will pay 25 percent more in bonus dollars.

Step 4: Working with CEO team goals and objectives session

The senior leadership is now ready to develop the action plans meant to achieve the three organizational goals shown above. At the end of the working session, the XPeGoals matrix reflects the deliverables for each area.

XPeGoals Example Inc. CEO Level		KPI and Targets Deadline: end of Q1		
Goal What?	Scope How?	Target	Stretch Target	Max Bonus Level
Positive EBT (Earnings Before Tax)	→ Optimize G&A → Retention of key staff → Increase sales revenue → Effective marketing spending → Competitive price control → Support systems stability	reach $5M EBT	$5.5M	125%
Positive cash flow	→ Cash flow management → Competitive price control → Capital expenditures control → Dynamic sourcing	reach $15M positive cash flow	$16.5M	125%
Increase market share	→ Increase cust sat levels → Increase market penetration → Increase quality	increase market share by 1 percentage point - to 8.9%	9.00%	125%

Fig. 25.4. Senior leadership team's working session results: goals and objectives are set.

Step 5: Aligning company goals.

With that out of the way, now it is time to prepare for the senior leadership team's alignment: in short, the CEO's direct reports and their reports. For that, we use the CEO's goals as alignment indexes—the indices of the cross-functional alignment—regardless of level. We insert three columns that will show, on all departmental goals matrix forms, the key deliverables for the entire organization, as they are reflected on the CEO-level matrix. These index columns will allow us to quickly identify alignment and to sort by goal.

Here is how that would look:

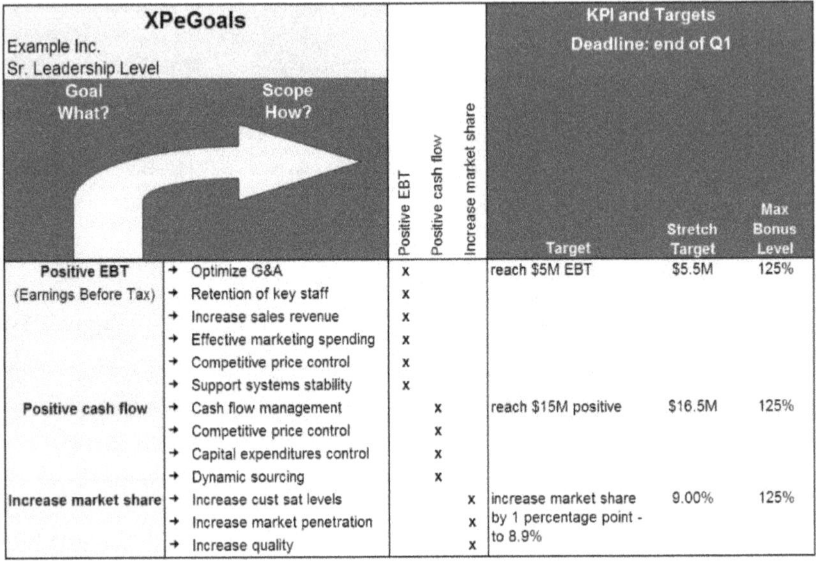

XPeGoals Example Inc. Sr. Leadership Level Goal What?	Scope How?	Positive EBT	Positive cash flow	Increase market share	KPI and Targets Deadline: end of Q1 Target	Stretch Target	Max Bonus Level
Positive EBT (Earnings Before Tax)	→ Optimize G&A	x			reach $5M EBT	$5.5M	125%
	→ Retention of key staff	x					
	→ Increase sales revenue	x					
	→ Effective marketing spending	x					
	→ Competitive price control	x					
	→ Support systems stability	x					
Positive cash flow	→ Cash flow management		x		reach $15M positive	$16.5M	125%
	→ Competitive price control		x				
	→ Capital expenditures control		x				
	→ Dynamic sourcing		x				
Increase market share	→ Increase cust sat levels			x	increase market share by 1 percentage point - to 8.9%	9.00%	125%
	→ Increase market penetration			x			
	→ Increase quality			x			

Fig. 25.5. Introducing CEO level goals as organizational priorities—to ensure alignment at all levels—the indices of company-wide goals alignment.

As stated before, all business units will be contributing, therefore all department leaders should align with these goals. Activities that are not in alignment with company goals should not exist. This is the final XPeGoals matrix for the leadership team's goals and objectives session, identifying all contributing business units and their leaders:

XPeGoals Example Inc. Sr. Leadership Level Goal What?	Scope How?	VP Operations	VP Sales	VP Marketing	VP Support	CIO	CFO	Positive EBT	Positive cash flow	Increase market share	KPI and Targets Deadline: end of Q1 Target	Stretch Target	Max Bonus Level
Positive EBT	→ Optimize G&A							x			reach $5M EBT	$5.5M	125%
	→ Retention of key staff							x					
	→ Increase sales revenue							x					
	→ Effective marketing spending							x					
	→ Competitive price control							x					
	→ Support systems stability							x					
Positive cash flow	→ Cash flow management								x		reach $15M positive	$16.5M	125%
	→ Competitive price control								x				
	→ Capital expenditures control								x				
	→ Dynamic sourcing								x				
Increase market share	→ Increase cust sat levels									x	increase market share by 1 percentage point - to 8.9%	9.00%	125%
	→ Increase market penetration									x			
	→ Increase quality									x			

Fig. 25.6. Identifying and naming the key contributors.

Step 6: Identifying contributors and their contributions.

By using the XPeGoals matrix, the goals and objectives working session becomes a team exercise in which for each line we answer the following question, "Who is contributing to the delivery of this goal?" Then, all contributors are identified in the column bearing their name with an "x" for the respective goal.

For instance, the VP of Sales is contributing to the goal of reaching positive EBT. This is now his and his team's goal, in perfect alignment with the organization's goals. Leaving the leadership goals working session, the VP of Sales will repeat the exercise at his team's level, thus trickling down perfectly aligned goals, targets, deadlines, and bonus payout levels. The goals and objectives team exercise will allow constructive dialogue to happen around the realism of goals, methods to achieve, types of strategies to employ, concerns and fears, etc.

For simplification purposes, in our example, all goals are equally important; in some cases, a goal can weigh 70 percent, while other goals will share the remaining 30 percent. This is an important piece in performance reviews and bonus calculations, and the goal weighting has to be well-established at the start of the exercise. If the CEO's focus is 70 percent on cash management, this percentage must trickle down along with the actual goal. This allows perfectly aligned goals prioritization, or, respectively, succession (that is, first pour the asphalt, complete task, and then paint road signage).

Using only one operations path, we will work through the trickledown process at all levels.

The next image represents the completed XPeGoals matrix, as a result of the senior leadership team's working session. The VP of Operations knows precisely where he and his team will contribute.

XPeGoals Example Inc. Sr. Leadership Level											KPI and Targets Deadline: end of Q1		
Goal What?	Scope How?	VP Operations	VP Sales	VP Marketing	VP Support	CIO	CFO	Positive EBT	Positive cash flow	Increase market share	Target	Stretch Target	Max Bonus Level
Positive EBT	→ Optimize G&A	x	x	x	x	x	x	x			reach $5M EBT	$5.5M	125%
	→ Retention of key staff	x	x	x	x	x	x	x					
	→ Increase sales revenue	x	x	x			x	x					
	→ Effective marketing spending		x	x			x	x					
	→ Competitive price control			x		x	x	x					
	→ Support systems stability				x	x		x					
Positive cash flow	→ Cash flow management	x	x	x	x	x	x		x		reach $15M positive	$16.5M	125%
	→ Competitive price control		x	x	x	x	x		x				
	→ Capital expenditures control				x	x	x		x				
	→ Dynamic sourcing				x	x	x		x				
Increase market share	→ Increase cust sat levels	x	x	x	x	x				x	increase market share by 1 percentage point - to 8.9%	9.00%	125%
	→ Increase market penetration		x	x	x					x			
	→ Increase quality	x			x	x				x			

Fig. 25.7. Identifying which goals each contributor will participate in achieving.

Step 7: Trickling down one level: setting goals and objectives for the Operations team.

The VP of Operations will start preparing his team's working session, by eliminating goals that Operations is unable to contribute to and allowing the team members to focus on the ones they control. To do so, he will change the XPeGoals matrix as follows:

- The items on the main goals column will be replaced with the lines marked with an "x" on the matrix shown in Fig. 25.7.
- The leadership team's names in the header will be replaced with the Operations management team's names, thus bringing the matrix one level down.

Step 7.1: Filtering the goals applicable to the Operations team: By applying an auto filter and selecting "x" under the "VP Operations" cell, we select the goals to which the Operations team will contribute.

XPeGoals
Example Inc.
Sr. Leadership Level

Goal What?	Scope How?	VP Operations	VP Sales	VP Marketing	VP Support	CIO	CFO	Positive EBT	Positive cash flow	Increase market share	KPI and Targets Deadline: end of Q1 Target	Stretch Target	Max Bonus Level
Positive EBT	→ Optimize G&A	x	x	x	x	x	x	x			reach $5M EBT	$5.5M	125%
	→ Retention of key staff	x	x	x	x	x	x	x					
	→ Increase sales revenue	x	x	x			x	x					
Positive cash flow	→ Cash flow management	x	x	x	x	x	x		x		reach $15M positive cash flow	$16.5M	125%
Increase market share	→ Increase cust sat levels	x	x	x	x	x				x	Increase market share by 1 percentage point - to 8.9%	9.00%	125%
	→ Increase quality	x			x	x				x			

Fig. 25.8. Identifying the goals for the Operations team.

Step 7.2: We are now preparing the **XPeGoals** matrix for the Operations team goals and objectives exercise, by changing goals to Operations team level, and contributors to Operations team managers:

XPeGoals
Example Inc.
Operations Team Level

Goal What?	Scope How?	Shipping Director	Returns Mgr	Service Ops Director	Order Entry Mgr	Warranty Mgr	QA Director	Positive EBT	Positive cash flow	Increase market share	KPI and Targets Deadline: end of Q1	Baseline Levels As of Q4 LY	Q1 Target Levels	Stretch Target	Max Bonus Level
Optimize G&A	→							x							
	→							x							
	→							x							
Retention of key staff	→							x							
	→							x							
	→							x							
	→							x							
	→							x							
Increase sales revenue	→							x							
	→							x							
	→							x							
Cash flow management	→								x						
	→								x						
	→								x						
Increase cust sat levels	→									x					
	→									x					
	→									x					
Increase quality	→									x					
	→									x					
	→									x					

Fig. 25.9. Preparing the XPeGoals matrix for the Operations team's goals and objectives working session.

Step 7.3: Operations team's goals and objectives working session. Just like in the case of the leadership team, the Operations team is now going to figure out together how they can achieve the goals, and which metrics and targets, if achieved, will contribute in fair part to the company targets in terms of cash, profitability, and market share. This is also where stretch goals and bonus payout levels are set.

Again, the two questions they need to answer is “How?” and “Who?” Note the maintained alignment with the overall company goals to identify which corporate-level goal the operations-level goal will contribute to. It is useful to capture reference—or baseline—levels for the target values of each KPI. We want to increase sales by 10 percent—applied to which value?

After the Operations team has completed its working session, their completed XPeGoals matrix looks like this:

XPeGoals Example Inc. Operations Team Level											KPI and Targets Deadline: end of Q1				
Goal What?	Scope How?	Shipping Director	Returns Mgr	Service Ops Director	Order Entry Mgr	Warranty Mgr	QA Director	Positive EBT	Positive cash flow	Increase market share	KPI and Targets Deadline: end of Q1	Baseline Levels As of Q4 LY	Q1 Target Levels	Stretch Target	Max Bonus Level
Optimize G&A	Restructure head office functions	x	x	x	x	x	x	x			reduce Ops G&A by 35%	$ 13.54 M	$ 8.81 M	$ 8.0 M	125%
	Reduce office space footprint	x	x	x	x	x	x	x							
	Renegotiate all support and maintenance services	x		x	x			x							
Retention of key staff	Employee engagement	x	x	x	x	x	x	x			95% retention for key staff	83%	95%	98.00%	125%
	Career path	x	x	x	x	x	x	x							
	Bonus program	x	x	x	x	x	x	x							
	Competitive pay	x	x	x	x	x	x	x							
	Stock grants	x	x	x	x	x	x	x							
Increase sales revenue	Reduce returns	x	x	x	x	x	x	x			returns down by 10% to 5.5%	6.10%	5.50%	5.00%	125%
	Increase order entry conversion rate			x	x			x			conversion up by 5% to 82%	77%	82%	90%	125%
	Increase NPS	x	x	x	x	x	x	x			NPS up by 20 points to 35	15	35	38.5	150%
Cash flow management	Increase labor efficiency	x	x	x	x		x		x		cost per labor hours down by 15%	$21.35	$18.15	$17.50	125%
	Optimize service cost	x	x	x	x				x		cost per processed unit down by 15%	$7.89	$6.70	$6.40	125%
	Six Sigma cost savings initiatives			x		x	x		x						
Increase cust sat levels	Decrease shipping delays	x								x	shipping delay down by 10% to 18h	19.8h	18h	15h	125%
	Increase service levels in CS and OE			x	x					x	SL increase to 80% at 90s	71%	80%	85%	125%
	Optimize packaging and recycle	x								x	reduction in packaging cost by 15%	$2.65	$2.25	$2.10	125%
Increase quality	Decrease missing and wrong	x			x					x	M&W down by 25%	2.35%	1.76%	1.60%	125%
	Supplier quality initiatives					x	x			x	Defect rate down by 20% to 3.5%	4.20%	3.50%	2.50%	125%
	Reduce damaged in transit	x								x	DIT down by 25% to 0.05%	0.063%	0.050%	0.03%	125%

Fig. 25.10. XPeGoals matrix showing the results of the goals and objectives working session for the Operations team, identifying contributors for each deliverable.

Now is the turn of the order entry manager, as we take yet another step in our exercise. She has everything she needs to continue the aligned trickle-down process of goals and objectives, down to her team’s level. Repeating all the steps above, she will prepare the XPeGoals matrix for her team working session.

As we follow through the levels of the organization, the team’s role is increasingly tactical. Regardless, down to the entry-level worker, we now have clearly defined and aligned goals and objectives, with metrics, targets, and bonus goals, assigned to each leader and team member. The XPeGoals matrix, at team leader level, for example, will have part of the goals shared by the team leader and the workers in her team, while the other half would be her own tactical goals as deliverables.

The Benefits of XPeGoals Methodology

- ✓ Quick agreement on goals and objectives through the entire organization.
- ✓ Little time spent in meetings to secure communication, buy-in, and/or alignment.
- ✓ Solid base for data-driven performance management.
- ✓ Solid base for rewards and recognition programs, career path, and merit increases.
- ✓ High employee engagement levels, synergy among and within teams.
- ✓ No disputes, misalignment, or lack of focus.
- ✓ No lack of prioritization, or conflicting goals left unaddressed.
- ✓ Improved team atmosphere and ownership of goals, through an empowered, collaborative team environment.

Chapter 26
Performance Reviews

The XPeGoals matrix sets the stage for an innovative approach to performance reviews, one that ensures most grievances in the area of performance management are addressed successfully. This innovative approach is a methodology called XPePerform (for Expedient Performance). The main improvement brought by XPePerform is around the impartiality and consistency of the reviews: if you are good at what you are doing, and can deliver the results you have been tasked to deliver, it will show up on your review, unaltered. With all the good consequences—merit increases, bonuses, career path—or the bad ones, there is unequivocal, undisputable feedback, and corrective action planning about poor performance.

Each company handles performance reviews in its own way, as influenced by the company's culture, ways of setting goals and objectives, and flavor of the day. One of the most common yet controversial performance review practices out there is the forced ranking—also known as the bell curve distribution. Based on the observation that given any random group of employees, some will exceed expectations (10–20 percent), the majority will perform at expectations (65–75 percent), and the rest will underperform (10–15 percent), the practice requires that the actual employee reviews in any team or department fall under this distribution. Hence, the name "forced." This method comes with few benefits and many disadvantages. We will explore a few of the most common beliefs about this methodology, examining the behaviors it drives as a practice, especially when it is misused.

Forced Ranking Myths and Reality

Myth: Forced ranking represents an easier way to manage and justify selections for layoffs.

Reality: This might have some limited value for the first round of layoffs that takes place in an organization, if the layoffs are not exceeding 10–15 percent of the workforce. It is a safe assumption to believe that in any team there are a few underperforming employees, and, in their case, the "below expectations" review will land their names on the layoff list in fair and true representation of their performances. After eliminating these underperforming employees, the following review will be faced by competent, "meets expectations" employees, out of which some will be "forced" down, to satisfy the requirements of this practice.
Yes, but how do we choose who is getting the undeserved "below expectations" review, followed by the ax on the next layoff list? Ideally, we would rank our employees from best to worst, and just pick the worst. In reality though, most managers will pick those who they would be ok to see laid off. It could be an employee who has a function that could be easily outsourced (regardless of the employee's performance), or, in case of a tie, an employee who might be a good performer by commonly accepted standards, but is not well-liked by the manager. Here's how, in real life, forced ranking can become a favoritism tool, allowing layoffs to be, in some cases, based, at least in some part, on subjective criteria.

Myth: Forced ranking will ensure not only the top performers get the attention of their leaders.

Reality: Simply put—not true. This practice will create the tools needed by employers to eliminate safely the bottom 10 percent of our lists, as many times and as frequently they might wish to do so. All the employees in the "meets expectations" category will live in constant fear of landing a "below expectations" review and securing a place on the dreaded layoff list. Constantly removing the bottom 10 percent of the list is not motivating the rest of the team at all. It hits the worst in the people-managers area, where the management level employees, well aware of how this practice works, will be a high turnover risk at all times. Therefore, instead of having employees focused on critical deliverables and pulling together, the effect of this practice seems to be the constant struggle to prove that someone else deserves the place at the bottom of the list—also known as "throwing people under the bus" or "backstabbing." The truly dangerous aspect of this "throwing people under the bus" as a survival method, is how wildly contagious it can become. Survival mechanisms in groups are instinctively based on learning from other group members' success in survival, and emulating the successful method used by others, in order to survive. If the company's culture allows this wildfire to spread, soon it can become common practice, to the detriment of performance, team spirit, and trust.

Myth: Forced ranking will ensure managers deal with poor performance.

Reality: Although designed to have this effect, in some cases this practice has an unexpected opposite effect. Ideally, without any layoffs at the horizon, the manager will work with the underperforming employee, and develop an action plan that guides the employee into meeting expectations. In this ideal case, the employee either becomes a good performer, or, through the performance management steps, is terminated without the umbrella of a layoff. In reality, as managers know that the "below expectations" employees will be terminated at the following round of layoffs, they will "save" the underperforming employee for that time.

For example, let's say Janet, the order entry manager at Example Inc., has a team of ten people. One is a bad performer, but the rest are great. Layoffs are not yet announced, but they will happen for sure—it's in the air. If Janet starts the corrective action process for her problem employee, she might find herself in a position to terminate him for cause before the layoffs kick in. At which point, she will then become forced to sacrifice a good performer—and she needs all those to meet the department goals. The solution? "Save" the underperforming employee for later, to be used in case of a layoff.

Myth: Forced ranking will ensure managers have clear and fair guidelines in giving bonuses, merit increases, and promotions.

Reality: Definitely intended to deliver exactly that, the practice can provide the visibility needed to create a good forecast as to what the future payroll should be planned for. Therefore, it is a great forecasting tool, in terms of payroll and bonus dollars. Beyond that, the same subjectivity and favoritism could be happening on the top end of the ranked list, just like with the bottom end.

Myth: Forced ranking is motivating all employees to do their best.

Reality: Untrue. Once the suspicion of favoritism and the realization that results do not really matter have taken hold of employee morale, the recovery is a hard one. The trust in the company's leadership could be seriously affected on all levels, in addition to the open and honest dialogue. The overall atmosphere is one of distrust, disengagement, and powerlessness.

Here is a interesting quote from an employee in such an environment, "I am not disputing my review any more—I learned my lesson. Last year I learned that results don't make a difference. By challenging the review, I just made him mad at me and made things even worse. Although I had exceeded all my goals and fully deserved an 'exceeds expectations', he just picked someone else for the forced ranking; he simply does not like me all that much. If I get a 'below expectations' I will appreciate the heads-up, and start looking for another job."

Another employee, finding himself in a similar case, stated with humor, "I don't need to improve all that much, right? It's like the old joke about the bear chasing a group of campers. I don't need to be running faster than the bear—just faster than the slowest camper in the group."

Myth: Forced ranking is recognizing and rewarding top performance.

Reality: Not quite so. What if Janet, our order entry manager, out of her team of ten employees, had four superstars? Would she be able to give all the raises and bonuses they deserve? Nope. She might get away with two—if the pressure exerted during calibration would not cause her to be left with only one. The rest of them would become frustrated, demotivated, and a turnover risk, hence, a loss for the company.

Myth: Departmental forced ranking should be depending on company results.

Reality: Absolutely the wrong thing to do. In some cases, direction is given to not allow too many "exceeds performance" ratings because the company, as a whole, is doing poorly. Even if, due to the financial situation of the company, no one will receive bonuses or merit increases, such a decision can have devastating morale effects on top contributors. Those who gave their best, to ensure the situation is not worse than it currently is, would perceive the decision as a slap in the face. The fact that sales were poor and the company is losing money should not cloud the innovative over-performance of the plant manager. Yet it does.

The Fix

There is, fortunately, a better way to manage, recognize, and reward performance, answering all open controversies and issues around the bell curve (forced ranking) system, or other, more traditional performance management methods in use. XPeGoals matrix creates the opportunity to address most of these shortfalls in a data-driven, undisputable manner. Its performance management utility, XPePerform, is built from the XPeGoals matrix by adding a few more columns to reflect actual results, performance rating, bonus levels, and the star or RYG (red-yellow-green) coding, as reflected in the weekly and monthly KPI charts.

Methodology—XPePerform

Using the same example from the previous chapter, at the end of Q1, for the Operations team, with the results entered, XPePerform looks like this:

XPePerform
Example Inc
Operations Team Level

Goal What?	Scope How?	Shipping Director	Returns Mgr.	Service Ops Director	Order Entry Mgr.	Warranty Mgr.	QA Director	KPI and Targets Deadline: end of Q1	Reference Levels As of Q4 LY	Q1 Target Levels	Stretch Target	Max Bonus Level	Actuals	Rating	Stars / RYG	Bonus Payout
Optimize G&A	→ Restructure HO functions	x	x	x	x	x	x	reduce Ops G&A by 35%	$ 13.54 M	$ 8.81 M	$ 8.0 M	125%	$7.71	EE	★★★	125%
	→ Reduce office space footprint	x	x	x	x	x	x									
	→ Renegotiate all support and maintenance services	x		x	x											
Retention of key staff	→ Employee engagement	x	x	x	x	x	x	95% retention for key staff	83%	95%	98.00%	125%	92%	BE	★	50%
	→ Career path	x	x	x	x	x	x									
	→ Bonus program	x	x	x	x	x	x									
	→ Competitive pay	x	x	x	x	x	x									
	→ Stock grants	x	x	x	x	x	x									
Increase sales revenue	→ Reduce returns	x	x	x	x	x	x	returns down by 10% to 5.5%	6.10%	5.50%	5.00%	125%	5.25%	ME	★★	100%
	→ Increase OE conv. rate			x	x			conversion up by 5% to 82%	77%	82%	90%	125%	91.50%	EE	★★★	125%
	→ Increase NPS	x	x	x	x	x	x	NPS up by 20 points to 35	15	35	38.5	150%	37	ME	★★	100%
Cash flow management	→ Increase labor efficiency	x	x	x	x		x	cost per labor hours down by 15%	$21.35	$18.15	$17.50	125%	$17.93	ME	★★	100%
	→ Optimize service cost	x	x	x	x			cost per processed unit down by 15	$7.89	$6.70	$6.40	125%	$6.68	ME	★★	100%
	→ 6S cost savings initiatives			x		x	x									
Increase cust sat levels	→ Decrease shipping delays	x						shipping delay down by 10% to 18h	19.8h	18h	15h	125%	17.5 hrs	ME	★★	100%
	→ Increase SL in CS and OE			x	x			SL increase to 80% at 90s	71%	80%	85%	125%	86.50%	EE	★★★	125%
	→ Optimize packaging & recycle	x						reduction in packaging cost by 15%	$2.65	$2.25	$2.10	125%	$2.24	ME	★★	100%
Increase quality	→ Decrease missing and wrong	x			x			M&W down by 25%	2.35%	1.76%	1.60%	125%	1.67%	ME	★★	100%
	→ Supplier quality Initiatives					x	x	Defect rate down by 20% to 3.5%	4.20%	3.50%	2.50%	125%	3.20%	ME	★★	100%
	→ Reduce damaged in transit	x						DIT down by 25% to 0.05%	0.063%	0.050%	0.03%	125%	0.052%	ME	★★	100%

Fig. 26.1. XPePerform for the Operations team, with end of Q1 results, star rating, and bonus levels.

We have the results of the quarter reflected in a manner that leaves zero room for interpretation, bias, or subjectivity. The same as for goals and objectives, the results will be made available at all levels, down to the individual contributor level, thus providing the performance-review data. In our example, all goals were equally weighted; therefore calculating bonus levels and performance rating is a simple average. In the case of weighted goals, we would use a weighted average.

As an exercise, let's find out what performance rating the VP of Operations should get for Q1. The bracket around the ME (meets expectations) rating, in our exercise, is +/- 10 percent. Contributors should not be deemed incompetent just because they are missing a decimal somewhere; neither do they walk on water by exceeding goals at the second decimal. The simple—or weighted—formula to calculate bonus percentage reflects the accuracy of this method. Applying it reversed, we obtain the qualitative performance rating. The VP of Operations, in our example, comes out at a bonus level of 102 percent (simple average for equally weighted goals), which places him at ME for Q1.

Quickly filtering the XPePerform matrix by individual contributions of the Operations leadership, we find that the shipping manager comes precisely at 98 percent bonus and ME rating, and the order entry manager at 103 percent bonus and ME rating.
In the next chapter, we will explore a weighted goals case study.

Here is how XPePerform looks like, sorted by the order entry manager's goals and results, with the calculated average in place.

XPePerform
Example Inc.
Operations Team Level

Goal What?	Scope How?	Shipping Director	Returns Mgr.	Service Ops Director	Order Entry Mgr.	Warranty Mgr.	QA Director	KPI and Targets Deadline: end of Q1	Reference Levels As of Q4 LY	Q1 Target Levels	Stretch Target	Max Bonus Level	Actuals	Rating	Stars / RYG	Bonus Payout
Optimize G&A	Restructure HO functions	x	x	x	x	x	x	reduce Ops G&A by 35%	$ 13.54 M	$ 8.81 M	$ 8.0 M	125%	$7.71	EE	***	125%
	Reduce office space footprint	x	x	x	x	x	x									
	Renegotiate all support and maintenance services	x		x	x											
Retention of key staff	Employee engagement	x	x	x	x	x	x	95% retention for key staff	83%	95%	98.00%	125%	92%	BE	*	50%
	Career path	x	x	x	x	x	x									
	Bonus program	x	x	x	x	x	x									
	Competitive pay	x	x	x	x	x	x									
	Stock grants	x	x	x	x	x	x									
Increase sales revenue	Reduce returns	x	x	x	x	x	x	returns down by 10% to 5.5%	6.10%	5.50%	5.00%	125%	5.25%	ME	**	100%
	Increase OE conv. rate			x	x			conversion up by 5% to 82%	77%	82%	90%	125%	91.50%	EE	***	125%
	Increase NPS	x	x	x	x	x	x	NPS up by 20 points to 35	15	35	38.5	150%	37	ME	**	100%
Cash flow management	Increase labor efficiency	x	x	x	x		x	cost per labor hours down by 15%	$21.35	$18.15	$17.50	125%	$17.93	ME	**	100%
	Optimize service cost	x	x	x	x			cost per processed unit down by 15%	$7.89	$6.70	$6.40	125%	$6.68	ME	**	100%
Increase cust sat levels	Increase SL in CS and OE			x	x			SL increase to 80% at 90s	71%	80%	85%	125%	86.50%	EE	***	125%
Increase quality	Decrease missing and wrong	x			x			M&W down by 25%	2.35%	1.76%	1.60%	125%	1.67%	ME	**	100%
														ME	**	103%

Fig. 26.2. XPePerform filtered by order entry manager's goals and results, with calculated bonus level and corresponding performance rating.

When presenting this methodology—combined, the XPeGoals matrix, together with XPePerform, the most common reaction it generates is, "Oh, so . . . it's that easy?" Well, yes it *is* that easy.

One of the objections to this method is, "How can you reflect the 'how' in someone's performance, how can you capture the behavior, team spirit, core competencies, etc?" If an employee has such bad behavior, or significant core competencies issues, it should be addressed immediately, not wait to be reflected somewhat at review time. If the issues are not major, then the only thing that should make a difference is results.

To our customers, the quality improvements in our product make more difference than the language the QA manager sometimes uses, especially when he thinks no one can hear him. The length of time someone waits on the line to speak to our agents is by far more important to that someone than the dress code adherence of the phone technician. Finally, reliable Internet download speed is what makes our neighbor happy, in total ignorance of the fact that the management style of the Fiber Optics team leader has upset the HR manager, at our local Internet service provider.

The principle behind the XPePerform is simple: results matter. In a company undergoing a turnaround, in need of immediate, clear results, and above average performance, using a straightforward, no-frills method for performance reviews will ensure exceptional engagement levels, and laser focus on results. Putting too much focus on the "how" could lead people to stray from the path of results to the path of office politics, if perceived as being the safest and quickest means of achieving professional success.

Here is some food for thought: would we even find ourselves in need of a turnaround if we had focused less on the "how," and more on palpable, unbiased, essential results? This methodology does not condone disrespectful behavior, verbal abuse, or unprofessional demeanor. Again, we should address such issues immediately, through proper behavioral corrective actions, rather than postpone them until performance review time. Thus leaving performance reviews dedicated entirely to achieving the desired results.

Chapter 27
Bonus Program

The first sacrificial offering on the altar of attempted recovery of a troubled business is the bonus and incentive program. The business is losing money, so we will not be paying any bonuses, we are not giving merit increases, and we are suspending our 401k and tuition reimbursement programs too. Makes sense? At first glance, maybe. After examining the consequences—definitely not.

Eliminating the bonus and incentive program has two important consequences: it demotivates employees, and it increases turnover.

Demotivation comes from the message we are putting out when suspending the bonus program; that message is, "We are no longer able and/or willing to recognize and reward good performance." Translated in most employees' reaction, whether acknowledged or not, this means, "It's ok to be mediocre, I won't be losing any money anyway," or "This year my performance review could well be average—will not make a difference on the paycheck," or even, "Why would I be working myself to the bone? There's nothing in it for me." No matter how self-motivated and dedicated an individual might be, everyone responds along the same lines to financial and non-financial rewards for performance—or lack thereof.

The second unwanted consequence of suspending the bonus program is the increased turnover of the best performers in the company. Overachievers are usually motivated by money, recognition, advancement, and are highly career-oriented. As they are usually quite confident in their ability to exceed expectations and score the highest bonus possible, they see this as a personal loss. They are also the most likely to remember what their initial contract stipulated—for example, $180,000 + 35 percent performance bonus—and to see the missing bonus as a unilateral breach of contractual terms, rather than a desperate maneuver to preserve some cash. They are the most likely to think along the lines of, "I just lost $63,000 a year due to this, so this is no longer a competitive employment offer for me. Elsewhere I'd get that money, or maybe even more." Finally, they are also the most likely employees to find more competitive employment opportunities fast—therefore, a high risk of turnover in the above average performance group of employees.

By removing the bonus program, we are generating two unwanted consequences: demotivate all employees and potentially lose our top performers. Definitely not good. However, due to the financial reality of the business, something needs to be done to preserve cash and cut costs.

During a turnaround execution, and post-turnaround stabilization, the success rate is in clear correlation with the turnaround project team's ability to execute as per plan and deliver the much-needed results fast. Therefore, it would make sense to reward and recognize performance quite aggressively. Quite the opposite of killing the bonus program, a bonus program geared toward key deliverables and milestones on the turnaround path, with frequent payouts, is more likely to generate the results we need. Including positive cash flow.

Based on the XPeGoals and XPePerform methodologies, this is quite easy to achieve. The following steps map the process of setting up an aggressive bonus program:

Establish Key Target Areas and Clearly Defined Goals

These key metrics are quite easy to pinpoint, based on the turnaround strategic plan, and the way the plan is reflected and trickled down throughout the organization, by means of the XPeGoals matrix. For illustration, using the health and beauty case study data we reviewed in the previous chapters, we know that the Example Inc. Operations team has to reduce operations general and administrative (G&A) costs by 35 percent before the end of first quarter. Achieving that will get each contributing team member 100 percent bonus payout for that particular KPI, for that particular period. If we should decide to have monthly bonus payouts, the road to the 35 percent G&A cost reductions can be mapped, based on the tactical plan behind the goal, and translated into monthly targets for the bonus payout. Here is the illustration of this example:

XPePerform Bonus Program						
Bonus Worksheet	Reference Levels	January Bonus Levels	February Bonus Levels	March Bonus Levels	Q1 Target Var +/-	Q1 Target Levels
Q1 KPI & Target	As of Q4	Mapping the Road for Monthly Payouts			+ / -	Target
Reduce Ops G&A by 35%	$ 13.54M	$ 12.5M	$10.5M	$ 8.81M	35%	$ 8.81M

Fig. 27.1. XPePerform bonus worksheet header with one sample line, mapping the monthly deliverable goal and path for bonus payout.

This example also demonstrates the methodology to reflect accurate starting and ending points as they pertain to goals, alignment, and bonus targets. Not only do we map the critical milestones and deliverables for each month end, but we also set a start point or reference level—usually the exit rate of the previous period—and an end point—expressed both in variation percentage, but also as an absolute measure. In the case illustrated above, we are saying that:

- Starting from a quarterly operations G&A cost of $13.54M, we need to achieve a reduction of this cost by 35 percent by the end of Q1.
- We need to reach a quarterly operations G&A cost of $8.80M or lower.
- These are the monthly milestones:
    - 7 percent reduction to be achieved by the end of January (net cost reduction of $0.95M).
    - 14 percent reduction in February (net reduction of $1.9M).
    - 14 percent to be achieved in March (the balance of $ 1.9M).

With this methodology applied across all the XPeGoals matrix targets, we are able to lay down the plan for all the deliverables of the Operations management team, complete with reference values—starting point, target variation, target end rates, and month-by-month milestones. Therefore, there can be no disputes about qualifying criteria for bonus, or the size of it.

XPePerform Bonus Program							
Bonus Worksheet	Reference Levels	January Bonus Levels	February Bonus Levels	March Bonus Levels	Q1 Target Var +/-	Q1 Target Levels	Q1 Stretch Target Levels
Q1 KPI & Target	As of Q4	Mapping the Road for Monthly Payouts			+ / -	Target	Stretch
Reduce Ops G&A by 35%	$ 13.54M	$ 12.5M	$10.5M	$ 8.81M	35%	$ 8.81M	$ 8.0M
95% retention for key staff	83%	87%	92%	95%	15%	95%	98%
Returns down by 10% to 5.5%	6.10%	5.90%	5.75%	5.50%	10%	5.50%	5.00%
Conversion up by 5% to 82%	77%	78%	80%	82%	5%	82%	90%
NPS up by 20 points to 35	15	19	27	35	20	35	38.5
Cost per labor hours down by 15%	$21.35	$20.50	$19.00	$18.15	15%	$18.15	$17.50
Cost per processed unit down by 15%	$7.89	$7.40	$7.00	$6.70	15%	$6.70	$6.40
Shipping delay down by 10% to 18h	19.8h	19.1h	18.5h	18h	10%	18h	15h
SL increase to 80% at 90s	71%	73%	77%	80%	12%	80%	85%
Reduction in packaging cost by 15%	$2.65	$2.50	$2.35	$2.25	15%	$2.25	$2.10
M&W down by 25%	2.35%	2.10%	1.90%	1.76%	25%	1.76%	1.60%
Defect rate down by 20% to 3.5%	4.20%	4.00%	3.75%	3.50%	20%	3.50%	2.50%
DIT down by 25% to 0.05%	0.063%	0.060%	0.055%	0.050%	25%	0.05%	0.03%

Fig. 27.2. XPePerform bonus worksheet with complete goals and target levels for monthly bonus payout—entire Operations team.

Make It a Multilevel Plan

Especially in the dynamic execution of a turnaround plan, but with great results in all environments, is the use of the multilevel bonus plan. This is how we motivate everyone to give their absolute best. Using the previous example, it would look like this:

XPePerform Bonus Program			
Bonus Worksheet	Q1 Bonus Levels		
Q1 KPI & Target	50%	100%	125%
Reduce Ops G&A by 35%	$ 9.5M	$ 8.81M	$ 8.0M

Fig. 27.3. XPePerform header with multilevel targets for one goal.

For a targeted variation of 35 percent on G&A cost, we are paying 100 percent of the agreed bonus level. Missing the target by one percentage point should not eliminate the bonus altogether; this could be a discouraging message in the case of aggressive target levels and drastic turnaround plans. Therefore, getting in the 90th percentile of the target value would lead to a payout of 50 percent in this case. Encouraging stretch performance, exceeding the goals by 10 percent would lead to bonus payouts of 125 percent. Using the same example, it all comes together as a multi-level bonus program (Fig. 27.4).

Going back to the XPeGoals matrix, now we can complete the matrix with the bonus target goals for our multilevel program. We can include the reference levels and the 50 percent payout target levels, which should be no less than 10 percent below the 100 percent target. Due to considerations for space and legibility, we have not done so in Fig. 27.4—several fields have been omitted.

XPePerform Bonus Program			
Bonus Worksheet	Q1 Bonus Levels		
Q1 KPI & Target	50%	100%	125%
Reduce Ops G&A by 35%	$ 9.5M	$ 8.81M	$ 8.0M
95% retention for key staff	92%	95%	98%
Returns down by 10% to 5.5%	5.75%	5.50%	5.00%
Conversion up by 5% to 82%	80%	82%	90%
NPS up by 20 points to 35	30	35	38.5
Cost per labor hours down by 15%	$19.25	$18.15	$17.50
Cost per processed unit down by 15%	$7.05	$6.70	$6.40
Shipping delay down by 10% to 18h	19h	18h	15h
SL increase to 80% at 90s	75.00%	80%	85%
Reduction in packaging cost by 15%	$2.45	$2.25	$2.10
M&W down by 25%	1.90%	1.76%	1.60%
Defect rate down by 20% to 3.5%	3.75%	3.50%	2.50%
DIT down by 25% to .05%	0.055%	0.050%	0.03%

Fig. 27.4. XPePerform bonus worksheet reflecting multilevel targets for all goals.

XPePerform Matrix
Example Inc.
Operations Team Level

Goal What?	Scope How?	Shipping Director	Returns Mgr.	Service Ops Director	Order Entry Mgr.	Warranty Mgr.	QA Director	KPI and Targets Deadline: end of Q1	Reference Levels As of Q4 LY	Q1 Target Levels 100% bonus payout	Stretch Target 125% bonus payout	Max Bonus Level	Actuals	Rating	Star / RYG	Bonus
Optimize G&A	Restrucure head office functions	x	x	x	x	x	x	reduce Ops G&A by 35%	$ 13.54 M	$ 8.81 M	$ 8.0 M	125%	$7.71	EE	***	125%
	Reduce office space footprint	x	x	x	x	x	x									
	Renegotiate all support and maintenance services	x		x	x											
Retention of key staff	Employee engagement	x	x	x	x	x	x	95% retention for key staff	83%	95%	98.00%	125%	92%	BE	*	50%
	Career path	x	x	x	x	x	x									
	Bonus program	x	x	x	x	x	x									
	Competitive pay	x	x	x	x	x	x									
	Stock grants	x	x	x	x	x	x									
Increase sales revenue	Reduce returns	x	x	x	x	x	x	returns down by 10% to 5.5%	6.10%	5.50%	5.00%	125%	5.25%	ME	**	100%
	Increase order entry conversion rate			x	x			conversion up by 5% to 82%	77%	82%	90%	125%	91.50%	EE	***	125%
	Increase NPS	x	x	x	x	x	x	NPS up by 20 points to 35	15	35	38.5	150%	37	ME	**	100%
Cash flow management	Increase labor efficiency	x	x	x	x		x	cost per labor hours down by 15%	$21.35	$18.15	$17.50	125%	$17.93	ME	**	100%
	Optimize service cost	x	x	x	x			cost per processed unit down by 15%	$7.89	$6.70	$6.40	125%	$6.68	ME	**	100%
	Six Sigma cost savings initiatives			x		x	x									
Increase cust sat levels	Decrease shipping delays	x						shipping delay down by 10% to 18h	19.8h	18h	15h	125%	17.5 hrs	ME	**	100%
	Increase service levels in CS and OE			x	x			SL increase to 80% at 90s	71%	80%	85%	125%	86.50%	EE	***	125%
	Optimize packaging and recycle	x						reduction in packaging cost by 15%	$2.65	$2.25	$2.10	125%	$2.24	ME	**	100%
Increase quality	Decrease missing and wrong	x			x			M&W down by 25%	2.35%	1.76%	1.60%	125%	1.67%	ME	**	100%
	Supplier quality initiatives					x	x	Defect rate down by 20% to 3.5%	4.20%	3.50%	2.50%	125%	3.20%	ME	**	100%
	Reduce damaged in transit	x						DIT down by 25% to 0.05%	0.063%	0.050%	0.03%	125%	0.052%	ME	**	100%

Fig. 27.5. XPePerform reflecting all results, performance, star rating, and bonus payout levels for the Operations team.

Showing in detail the actual result values and the bonus payout levels, XPePerform loaded with bonus payout levels and actual results for Q1 looks like this:

XPePerform Weighted Bonus Program

Bonus Worksheet	Reference Levels	Q1 Bonus Levels			Actuals	Payout Level
Q1 KPI & Target	As of Q4 2008	50%	100%	125%	Absolute	Equal Weighting
Reduce Ops G&A by 35%	$ 13.54 M	$ 9.5 M	$ 8.81 M	$ 8.0 M	$7.71	125%
95% retention for key staff	83%	92.00%	95%	98.00%	92.15%	50%
Returns down by 10% to 5.5%	6.10%	5.75%	5.50%	5.00%	5.25%	100%
Conversion up by 5% to 82%	77%	80%	82%	90%	91.50%	125%
NPS up by 20 points to 35	15	30	35	38.5	37	100%
Cost per labor hours down by 15%	$21.35	$19.25	$18.15	$17.50	$17.93	100%
Cost per processed unit down by 15%	$7.89	$7.05	$6.70	$6.40	$6.68	100%
Shipping delay down by 10% to 18h	19.8h	19h	18h	15h	17.5 hrs	100%
SL increase to 80% at 90s	71%	75.00%	80%	85%	86.50%	125%
Reduction in packaging cost by 15%	$2.65	$2.45	$2.25	$2.10	$2.24	100%
M&W down by 25%	2.35%	1.90%	1.76%	1.60%	1.67%	100%
Defect rate down by 20% to 3.5%	4.20%	3.75%	3.50%	2.50%	3.20%	100%
DIT down by 25% to .05%	0.063%	0.055%	0.050%	0.03%	0.052%	100%
Total Payout:						**101.92%**

Fig. 27.6. XPePerform detail showing bonus levels, results, and bonus payout for the Operations team.

The example studied above assumed all goals are equally important. What if that is not the case? Being that Example Inc. is undergoing a customer-centric turnaround, the most important goals are cash and customer satisfaction related. How would XPeGoals and XPePerform reflect that? Quite simple. By adding a goal-weight column and introducing the weighting factors in all formulas, as shown in Fig. 27.7.

XPePerform Weighted Bonus Program								
Bonus Worksheet	Reference Levels	Q1 Bonus Levels			Actuals	Weight	Bonus Payout	
Q1 KPI & Target	As of Q4 2008	50%	100%	125%	Absolute	Goal Weight	Level	With Goal Weighting
Reduce Ops G&A by 35%	$ 13.54 M	$ 9.5 M	$ 8.81 M	$ 8.0 M	$7.71	25.00%	125%	31.25%
95% retention for key staff	83%	92.00%	95%	98.00%	92.15%	2.50%	50%	1.25%
Returns down by 10% to 5.5%	6.10%	5.75%	5.50%	5.00%	5.25%	2.50%	100%	2.50%
Conversion up by 5% to 82%	77%	80%	82%	90%	91.50%	2.50%	125%	3.13%
NPS up by 20 points to 35	15	30	35	38.5	37	40.00%	125%	50.00%
Cost per labor hours down by 15%	$21.35	$19.25	$18.15	$17.50	$17.93	2.50%	100%	2.50%
Cost per processed unit down by 15%	$7.89	$7.05	$6.70	$6.40	$6.68	2.50%	100%	2.50%
Shipping delay down by 10% to 18h	19.8h	19h	18h	15h	17.5 hrs	2.50%	100%	2.50%
SL increase to 80% at 90s	71%	75.00%	80%	85%	86.50%	10.00%	125%	12.50%
Reduction in packaging cost by 15%	$2.65	$2.45	$2.25	$2.10	$2.24	2.50%	100%	2.50%
M&W down by 25%	2.35%	1.90%	1.76%	1.60%	1.67%	2.50%	100%	2.50%
Defect rate down by 20% to 3.5%	4.20%	3.75%	3.50%	2.50%	3.20%	2.50%	100%	2.50%
DIT down by 25% to .05%	0.063%	0.055%	0.050%	0.03%	0.052%	2.50%	50%	1.25%
Total Payout:								116.88%

Fig. 27.7. XPePerform detail showing bonus levels, results, and bonus payout on weighted goals.

In this case, because the Operations team has achieved good results primarily in the higher weight goals, and missed its targets in lower weight goals, the overall performance rating and bonus payout reflect the Operations team performance at an 116.88 percent bonus payout, corresponding to an exceeds expectations (three-star) rating.

Pay Frequently—Monthly or Quarterly

If employees are at risk of doubting the financial stability of the company, that is a good incentive to start rebuilding trust by monthly bonus payouts. There is nothing worse for morale and enthusiasm in a company than a bonus program that employees do not honestly believe in, or fear the company will be closed by the payout date. As employers, we expect immediate results; we should be making immediate payments, to keep the results coming.

Don't Break Your Promise

It's not uncommon to hear a manager say, "When we set up the targets we were almost finished; we never thought we'd come out of it and that we would actually be able to reach these numbers. Now we need them adjusted higher," as a justification of changing the rules right in the middle of the game. This is a big no-no. You asked for performance, you got it, you need to pay for it. It would not be fair to change your mind halfway through, and make it impossible for people to reach their goals.

There is nothing wrong with setting targets that are more ambitious next quarter, but, if you have started this quarter setting up a goal for a bonus program and employees made it happen, they need to be paid for it. Our employees should not live under the impression that they are chasing moving targets, or that they can never be "good enough."

Don't Get Greedy

Sometimes bonus programs are twisted in the middle of the game to try to accomplish more. An example of such a twist applied to an otherwise good bonus plan could be to delay payment on it and condition it on staying employed with the company for another X number of months. While it could be thought to be a good idea to increase retention, the results of such a twist could be:

- Demotivation, due to increased concerns regarding the company's "real" cash-flow situation, as some employees could perceive this maneuver as an attempt to delay a payment.
- Increased turnover, due to concerns regarding employees' job security, as employees could read it as, "Oh, they're probably going to lay off half of us until then anyway."
- Concerns regarding future bonus programs, due to the idea that they could be changed midway so they would not be paid after all; the manipulative aspect of this twist could lead to employee frustration.
- Lack of trust in leadership, due to obvious integrity issues.

Furthermore, the type of performance and aggressive goals set in the example above cannot be realistically expected to continue on an ongoing basis. No one can operate in crisis mode and hope to achieve stability. After the execution of the operational plan, and the subsequent stabilization, goals should reflect more moderate, ambitious yet achievable values, corresponding to continuous improvement strategies.

After achieving operational excellence, the targets should reflect the aim to achieve stable, profitable, customer-centric operating performance, geared toward continuous improvement rather than dramatic changes.
In conclusion, a bonus program, just like any other program we would be launching in a business, needs to have well-defined goals. What do we want to achieve? We want to realign the organization, at all levels, on delivering goals that lead to profitability. Later on, we can examine the results and find out what is working and what is not, if it needs adjusting, and so on. The quick key to a successful bonus program remains: make it aggressive enough to make a difference, with frequent payouts, and clear, ambitious-yet-achievable deliverables.

Chapter 28
Cross-Functional Visibility: Scorecards and Dashboards

The entire organization is now aligned, motivated, in complete understanding of what the deliverables are, and ready for action. As we start executing the turnaround plan, all levels in the organization should be kept up-to-date with the progress, achievements, and delays.

Everyone is, more or less, aware of his or her own achievements, as an individual, and as an immediate team. However, in most cases, employees cannot visualize the big picture, see how other teams are performing, and find out how the company is progressing along the path to recovery.

Using the methodologies described in previous chapters, putting together an information vehicle becomes quite accessible. With an insignificant time investment, the monthly review scorecards can be fitted to be displayed and/or circulated throughout the organization. Using the same example as before, and starting from the XPeGoals matrix and the goals and targets established therein, we start by building the monthly scorecard. For cross-functional reporting purposes, the detailed "how" and "who" have no relevance, as we are trying to capture the performance of business units versus plan.

Performance Scorecard			
Example Inc.			
Leadership Team	KPI and Targets As of March 31	Actuals	Star
Positive EBT	reach $5M EBT	$5.5M	★★★
Positive cash flow	reach $15M positive cash flow	$7.2M	★
Increase market share	increase market share by 1 percentage point - to 8.9%	8.70%	★★

Fig. 28.1. Performance scorecard reflecting company performance on key company goals.

Not by accident, our example reflects some below-target results, in an area of high concern—cash. In many cases, the good intent behind communicating results throughout the organization is hindered by the concern regarding the employees' reaction to seeing the underperformance in one area or another, leading to decisions against open communication of results. The counterpoint here is that employees will not focus on fixing an issue if they have no idea the issue needs fixing. If cash is short and everyone knows it, expenses will be more carefully scrutinized and approved, payments will be sent out with slight delays, and everyone will pull together toward achieving the goal.

As for potential employee concerns with regard to the financial stability of the company, these should also be addressed with candor and resolve, "Yes, we have an issue, this is why we have the issue, we are working on fixing it by doing these things, and we expect it to be under control before the end of next month." Open and honest communication about underperforming areas will ensure employee cohesion and focus. The struggling business unit will feel supported and motivated to push harder than ever before.

A big caveat though—especially in publicly traded companies: the communication might touch sensitive areas, therefore, all audiences must be educated as to the confidentiality of the information made available. Timing the communication is also a good way to mitigate confidentiality risks. If company performance will be made public on the 23rd of each month, for example, we can communicate all details deemed necessary the next morning.

With all these considerations in mind, we can proceed to communicate the performance of key areas of the business: sales, operations, IT, etc. Our operations example shown in the previous chapters will set the ground for another relevant performance scorecard, at the department level.

Performance Scorecard				
Example Inc.		*As of March 31st*		
Operations Team				
		KPI and Targets	Actuals	Star / RYG
Optimize G&A	→	reduce Ops G&A by 35%	$7.71	★★★
Retention of key staff	→	95% retention for key staff	92%	★
Increase sales revenue	→	returns down by 10% to 5.5%	5.25%	★★
	→	conversion up by 5% to 82%	91.50%	★★★
	→	NPS up by 20 points to 35	37	★★
Cash flow management	→	cost per labor hours down by 15%	$17.93	★★
	→	cost per processed unit down by 15%	$6.68	★★
Increase cust sat levels	→	shipping delay down by 10% to 18h	17.5 hrs	★★
	→	SL increase to 80% at 90s	86.50%	★★★
	→	reduction in packaging cost by 15%	$2.24	★★
Increase quality	→	M&W down by 25%	1.67%	★★
	→	Defect rate down by 20% to 3.5%	3.20%	★★
	→	DIT down by 25% to 0.05%	0.052%	★★

Fig. 28.2. Performance scorecard reflecting team performance on goals.

What would be the best vehicles to communicate these performance scorecards? They could be emailed to everyone as PowerPoint presentations. They could be posted in print in common areas—kitchenettes, break rooms. They could be rotating on electronic wallboards, among other messaging, where available. Finally, they could be published on the company's Intranet. Regardless of the vehicle of choice for communication, the availability of the information is what makes the difference.

For a selected number of metrics, a perspective view is required. For these, a trend analysis chart should accompany the performance scorecard, if we want to present the evolution over time: the historic view, where we are, and—if needed—a future projection. In addition, trend analysis is allowing a deeper understanding of the drivers behind trends.

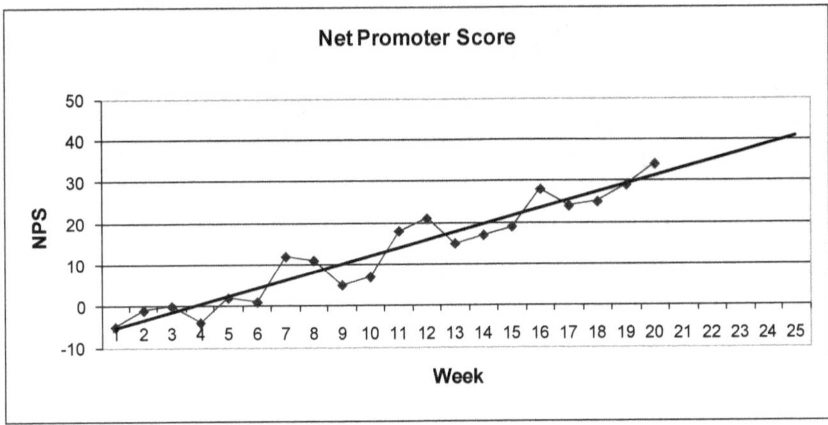

Fig. 28.3. Net promoter score results with trend line.

Cross-functional visibility is, ultimately, an accountability tool. There is no more room to "cover up" bad performance and build silo walls—each business unit owner has to answer for his or her team's poor performance.

In some areas, month-end results communication is not enough to ensure alignment and accountability through cross-functional visibility. Let us explore an example—problem statement plus fix.

Case Study

Example Inc. has a disconnect in the visibility of inventory levels, both at store level and in the customer-service contact center. Therefore, these areas will commit to two-day delivery lead times, while the ordered product is, in fact, backordered for weeks. The systemic fix for the issue is a major upgrade in technology—not something to have happen during a turnaround. However, there is a need of a patch-fix in the interim, due to the negative impact on customer satisfaction levels and rising cancelation rates.

The dashboard shown in Fig. 28.4 could be such a patch-fix, allowing all front-line channels to have access to information regarding exceptional situations. While it doesn't give inventory levels, normal delivery times are to be assumed unless the product is listed as backordered. In this situation, the front-line worker can inform the customer, set correct expectations, and offer similar products, if needed. It doesn't require daily updates—if everything is running normal then it sits empty—yet providing everyone the peace of mind that comes with knowledge, and the certainty behind it.

This example showed us how cross-functional visibility is helping with our customer-centric turnaround, with zero investment and almost-zero cost to maintain it. While it cannot constitute a permanent solution by itself, this type of simple, ultra-low cost, temporary fix will allow improved performance from financial—lower cancellation rates, lower complaints—and service quality perspectives, with the derived benefit of increased customer satisfaction.

Lead Time Dashboard

Example Inc.

Product / Range	Reason	Expected
Bubbly Shampoo 15floz	shipment delayed in customs	25-Apr
Night Cream, 2oz, Vanilla	major order influx due to BOGO promo	17-Apr
French Hair Accessories - all	hurricane caused delays for sea shipment	20-Apr
Key Areas:		
Central Distribution Center	Normal, no delays	
Canada DC	Normal, no delays	
East Coast DC	Limited impact due to weather, will ship Saturday to catch up	
Florida DC	Closed due to hurricane - 48 hrs delay until next Monday	20-Apr

ALERT! ALERT! ALERT!

- Cat 3 tropical storm causes major delays in all shipments on SE Coast.
- FL and TX regional distribution is suspended, stores closed.
- Inbound shipment from France is in holding pattern at sea.

Fig. 28.4. Lead time dashboard showing relevant information for front-line channels.

Chapter 29
Optimized Organizational Design

During a turnaround, the organizational structure undergoes serious change, mainly focused on rightsizing the organization to the declining sales volumes. However, this is an opportune moment to create the environment needed to reach another significant milestone on the path of stabilization and growth: self-managed teams.

In order for self-managed teams to perform and thrive, the environment and overall organizational culture have to provide the following:

- Clear goals and objectives, in perfect alignment with the organization's goals.
- Clear prioritization around these goals.
- An aggressive program for rewards and recognition.
- Career path.
- Clearly defined work flows, process flows, and escalation paths.
- Readily available information.
- Empowerment—complete with levels of authority and anti-abuse mechanisms.
- Support from the organization.

We will examine these one by one, as well as the solutions to achieve each one, in a synergized and cost-effective way.

Clear Goals and Objectives, In Perfect Alignment with the Organization's Goals

In Chapter 25, we examined closely the XPeGoals matrix, the method of choice to achieve clear goals and objectives. Perfect alignment is critical to the performance of self-managed teams because it allows team members to know what they should be focusing on, what the deliverables of each area of focus are, and how each team contributes to the entire organization's goals. By allowing individual contributors access to "the big picture," their contribution becomes a significant piece of a puzzle they now understand. It also allows the employees to have a sense of control—over their individual careers and the company's destiny. Therefore, the daily inputs from a manager are no longer needed to steer the focus and performance of the team; they all know what it is they are contributing to, how, and why.

Clear Prioritization around These Goals

The examples presented in Chapters 25 and 26 were illustrating priorities with equal weight. In other cases, goals can be assigned weights, thus clarifying the priority order in which the goals should be achieved, or where resources should be allocated.

An example, based on the case study in Chapter 27, would be for the Operations team to reduce G&A cost by 35 percent as a 75 percent weight goal, while the rest of the goals share equally the remaining 25 percent. By allowing G&A reductions to carry such a tremendous weight, we get everyone focused on G&A cost reductions first, and address the rest of the goals only after ensuring the main goal has been achieved. This also allows the team members to decide quickly and swiftly in cases of conflicting priorities, thus eliminating confusion, conflict, bad decisions, and escalations.

In other cases, goal prioritization has more to do with the timing of goals. The concrete foundation has to be poured first, after which the walls can be erected, while roofing comes last. In such cases, the XPeGoals matrix has to include the timing, duration, sequence, and deadline of each task—ideally by attaching a Gantt chart to it.

Regardless of the type of goals prioritization—equal, weighted, or sequential, the clarity around these goals brings the self-managed team the ability to self-manage successfully. This point, together with the one above, answers the self-managed team's question. "What do we need to accomplish?"

An Aggressive Program for Rewards and Recognition

Now we need to answer the question, "Why? What's in it for me?" For the sarcastic, dictatorial manager who'd answer, "Because it's your job," there's a caveat to consider: This is the path to mediocre performance, achieved by some discouraged, demotivated people; out of these, some have landed there in error or ignorance of such methods, and are looking to leave anyway. Such attitude toward what should motivate employees leads to the creation of hostage employee behaviors.

For the managers looking to achieve exceptional results, the path of motivation awaits. An equally ambitious rewards program must exist, designed to match the ambitious goals we are setting during a turnaround, and, afterward, during a period of post-turnaround stabilization and growth.

We examined rewards programs closely in Chapter 27. Part of the answer to the self-managed team's question. "Why?" should be, "Because not only do I get my salary paid on time, but I can also get a hefty bonus, one that makes a difference in my life."

Career Path

The other part of the answer to the self-managed team's question, "Why?" should be, "Because I can advance in this company, and I have personal growth opportunity matching my skills and interests."

One of the biggest benefits of the XPeGoals/XPePerform matrix system of setting goals and assessing results is the ability to identify precisely the top performers, even in a climate of (apparently) overall poor performance. Even if the company is losing money and considering bankruptcy, there might be overachievers who we would like to know about, engage, promote, and retain.

The existence of career paths linked directly to measured, hard performance is a powerful motivator for self-managed teams. All arguments are put aside, all pet peeves subside, and everyone is motivated to contribute their best. Not everyone will get the promotion, of course; this is the reality of the pyramidal structure of all organizations. The flatter the organization, the harder it will be to promote. However, the direct link between individual performance and promotability is at the core of individual motivation to succeed.

Clearly Defined Work Flows, Process Flows, and Escalation Paths

We are starting to answer the third and final question of self-managed teams, "How?" Documentation of work flows and processes is essential to ensure a standardized, high-quality, efficient, and consistent performance. Process maps are the starting point, together with the development of standard operating procedures (SOPs) that encompass all the process variables and do not allow for exceptions.

These process flows have to be geared to the audience, in terms of language and skill expectations. Building these is not a one-step process, as they require trials by fire to ensure that the final product is able to address all possibilities in an integrated, consistent manner.

Readily Available Information

All SOPs and all other information needed by employees to be successful in their jobs need to be readily available, in a system that does not constitute a challenge. Whether it's by means of the Intranet, a scripted knowledge base, or a customer-relationship management (CRM) system with all SOPs built-in, it matters less. Information management and availability represents a challenge, as we have to make sure all information made available to the employees is neither conflicting, nor obsolete. We want to be sure that it can be easily located.

Empowerment—Complete with Levels of Authority and Anti-Abuse Mechanisms

If employees are required to seek approval from their manager on every little thing they do—that's never going to become a self-managed team. Levels of empowerment can be a part of SOPs, ensuring that employees know precisely how far they can go when making a judgment call, an exception, or apply a credit to an account. In addition, they need to know what escalation path to follow in case their task exceeds their authority level.

Wherever there is front-line empowerment, there needs to exist some form of mechanism to ensure abuse will not happen. Examples of such mechanisms are not allowing access to a credit card account unless the account holder is on the line, not averaging more than $5 per account in discretionary credits, and not exceeding more than $25 per single account at the front-line bank teller level. These can be system settings—limiting the employee's ability to grant a credit higher than $25, as in our example. Alternatively, they can be reports, allowing to study behaviors and to run analyses on root causes and variation. A combination of both is ideal.

Support from the Organization

Finally, support from the organization is essential for the self-managed team's ability to succeed. Backed up by corresponding systems and processes, the self-managed team member does not require finding a manager to "smooth things over" or "make things happen." The self-managed team members must have a clear understanding about where to go for support, escalations, or direction. They also need to know what defines an emergency and how to react, whom to inform. Complete with training and development, the support for self-managed teams cannot lack in availability, open dialogue, and positive attitude—thus encouraging the teams to feel supported and to reach out when needed.

Last, but not least, leadership should develop a sense of trust in the successful employees and self-managed teams, and value their judgment, as it is demonstrated by their results. Leadership should engage the self-managed teams directly, in respect of their processes, rather than request work via the department head. Engaging teams top-down (via the department head) creates, for self-managed teams, an exception process—a process that is not a part of their charter, thus creating confusion and potentially generating errors. Should we handle this case differently—because it comes from the manager?

Self-managed teams are sustainable and long-term successful in a climate of clear definitions and stability. Once a team has proven to have the ability to function successfully as a self-managed team, the recipe should be preserved. The old adage, "Don't mess with perfection" comes to mind.

Stage 3
Stabilization

"Victory belongs to the most persevering."

~Napoleon Bonaparte (1769–1821)

Chapter 30
Wrapping Up a Successful Turnaround

What makes a successful turnaround? How can we define it, measure it—so we can recognize and celebrate the success? As with everything else, we need to go back to the original turnaround project plan and see if we have attained the goals we had at the beginning of the recovery effort.

A turnaround effort can be considered as successfully completed even if the company still carries debt. "Debt free" status is the next milestone on the path to stabilization and growth. Even if a relatively large amount of debt is still showing on the books, a turnaround effort can be considered successfully completed and stable if:

- Earnings before tax (EBT) is showing a comfortably positive number, with at least three consecutive data points.
- The positive EBT is achieved in a stable, long-term viable environment. In short, a company can only go for so long without most maintenance contracts, any capital expenditures, or employee benefits, for example. Some of these restrictive measures were implemented in order to buy time for the operational turnaround effort to start yielding results; however, they cannot be maintained long-term in a stable, competitive business environment. The same logic applies for the employee workload; for a while we might have decided to increase workload for existing employees to compensate for a restrictive payroll availability; however, this measure cannot be maintained long term.

- Finally, EBT has to show a growth trend—even if a moderate one. We are not out of the woods yet if EBT shows a couple of months of black, then visits red land for another couple of months, and so on.

There is a solid, complex reason why, throughout this book, we have looked at EBT rather than the more popular EBITDA (earnings before interest, tax, depreciation, and amortization). First, we have to keep a watchful eye on the company's ability to pay interest on the debt it carries. Second, removing depreciation and amortization does not paint the true picture of the company's ability to operate long term in profitability.

Going back to the initial operational turnaround project plan, we will get answers to two critical questions:

- Did we deliver on the plan's goals?
- Was it enough to ensure the return into stable profitability?

To refresh our memory, the original project plan for the multi-dealership car sales business looked like this:

EXPL—Current Org	EXPL—Future Design	Key Actions	Owner(s)
Headoffice overhead @ $12M	Headoffice overhead @ $4.9M	Reduce management headcount, redesign org, outsource backoffice functions	Jones (Stevens, Corey, Smith, Johnson)
Dealership count: 38	Dealership count: 16	Identify low performing locations and close; reassign / liquidate inventory	Adams (Benson, Evans, McDonnel)
-	Online sales division	Create, implement, staff	Samuel (Jameson, Schmidt)
In-house printing operation	-	Outsource	Johnson
Dealership level organization	Optimized, increased variability	Reduced fixed headcount, reassign tasks towards variable	Matthews (Stevens, Foley)
Inventory $72M	Inventory @ $30M	Organize close-out sales events, heavy promo, sell at cost	Trenton (Peterson, Phelps, Ricks)
Project Manager: Chris Jackson (XYZ Consulting)			
Documentation: Julie Anderson (x 5355), Annie Smithe (XYZ Consulting)			

Fig. 30.1. Initial operational turnaround plan.

We will now add to it a column of results.

EXPL—Current Org	EXPL—Future Design	Key Actions	Owner(s)	Results
Headoffice overhead @ $12M	Headoffice overhead @ $4.9M	Reduce management headcount, redesign org, outsource backoffice functions	Jones (Stevens, Corey, Smith, Johnson)	Reduced to $ 4.78M
Dealership count: 38	Dealership count: 16	Identify low performing locations and close; reassign / liquidate inventory	Adams (Benson, Evans, McDonnel)	All locations are now profitable: a total of 27 locations stayed open
-	Online sales division	Create, implement, staff	Samuel (Jameson, Schmidt)	Created, profitable in 60 days since inception date
In-house printing operation	-	Outsource	Johnson	Completed. Reduced printing costs by 57%
Dealership level organization	Optimized, increased variability	Reduced fixed headcount, reassign tasks towards variable	Matthews (Stevens, Foley)	All completed. 13 units successfully restructured, 3 closed
Inventory $72M	Inventory @ $30M	Organize close-out sales events, heavy promo, sell at cost	Trenton (Peterson, Phelps, Ricks)	Inventory reduced at $ 38 M. Renegotiated terms with manufacturers.
Documentation: Julie Anderson (x 5355), Annie Smithe (XYZ Consulting)				
Project Manager: Chris Jackson (XYZ Consulting)				

Fig. 30.2. Operational turnaround plan with results.

As we can see, not quite everything worked as planned.

1. Head office overhead costs reduction initiative exceeded plan by a little bit, finishing at $4.78M instead of a goal of $4.9M—a cost reduction of 60 percent over the initial spending number. Kudos for the Jones team!

2. Dealership count did not go down to 16—as originally planned. However, the team was able to make profitable 13 business units out of the original 16 that were proposed for the "restructure-make profitable" effort. Therefore, the team closed only nine units: six from the original list and three after they failed to become profitable through restructuring. These are significant results, as the company managed to maintain a larger presence on the market than originally believed possible, yet all business units turned a profit. Amazing . . .

3. The online sales division was created, implemented successfully at the head office, and broke even within 60 days. Awesome work!

4. In-house printing operation went away, replaced by carefully selected vendors under strict terms for quality, fulfillment time, and payments. Total expenses associated with the printing of marketing and store collaterals dropped by 57 percent.

5. The fifth team worked hard to restructure the 13 units and maintain them. A majority of this success was achieved through increased variability in the locations' workforce, aggressive rewards programs that compensated overachievement at any level, and a variety of cost reduction and avoidance initiatives. Team Matthews was instrumental and complementary at the same time with team Adams, enabling the dealership count restructuring team to save as much of the network as possible, and taking more on their plates than originally planned.

6. Team Trenton was unable to reduce inventory as per the target of $30M, mostly due to the fact that 13 more units that planned remained in business. However, the team compensated for this pseudo-miss by renegotiating payment and inventory ownership terms with the manufacturers, therefore achieving the underlining cash flow goal. creative work there . . .

Therefore, the answer to question 1, "Did we deliver on the plan's goals?" is a definite "Yes."

For the second question, we will analyze the revenue and net profit (loss) for EXPL Inc., before and after the operational turnaround.

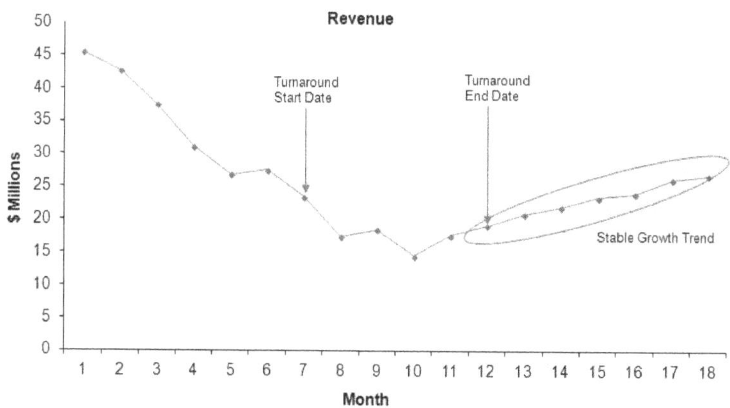

Fig. 30.3. Revenue by month analysis showing post-turnaround stable growth trend.

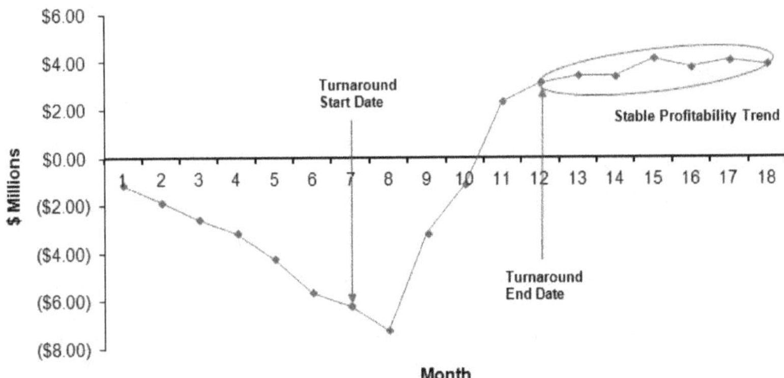

Fig. 30.4. Net profit (loss) by month analysis showing post-turnaround stable profitability trend.

Both charts reveal a significant, stable growth in both revenue and profitability. That will put the answer to the second question, "Was it enough to ensure the return into stable profitability?" as a "Yes."

In some cases, when the economy is severely recessed, the revenue trend will not show promise for a longer period of time. However, if the profit (loss) line shows stable—even if minimal—growth, although hard to achieve without a significant growth in revenue, it can be considered that, through significant increases in operational variability, we have a successful result of our turnaround action. The net profit has to be well into the positive for such a case, to ensure the cushion needed for volatile sales in a recessed economy.

Now let's see what an unstable result looks like on a chart.

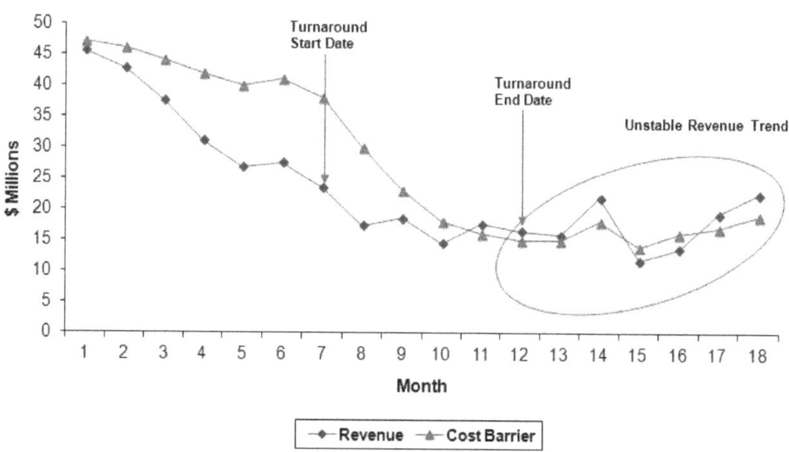

Fig. 30.5. Revenue vs. cost barrier by month analysis showing an unstable profitability trend.

In this case, the operational turnaround was able to achieve a drop in the cost barrier—or tipping point—value, allowing the company to be profitable at significantly lower revenue numbers. The revenue trend is unstable, crossing below the tipping point more than once. While this could be environmental or due to poor sales and marketing strategy and execution, the operational turnaround could continue the effort of further dropping the cost barrier. The cost barrier in our example shows a decreased gap between cost and revenue, as an illustration of the increased variability concept. In a truly variable environment, the cost barrier is the sum of two components: the fixed cost (a straight line) and the variable cost—therefore, not a straight line.

In this unstable revenue example, net profit (loss) reflects the same unstable behavior, with no discernible growth trend.

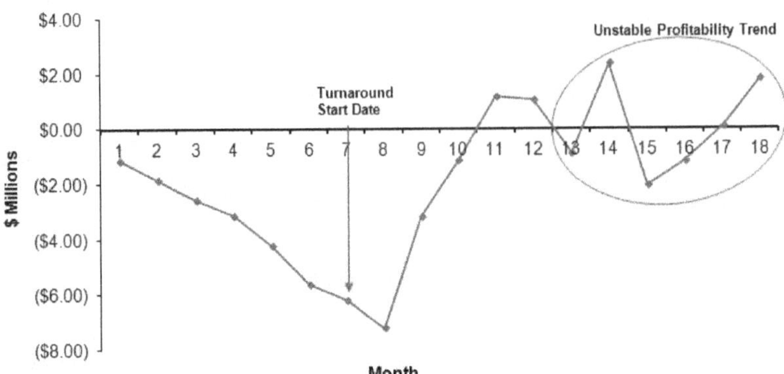

Fig. 30.6. Net profit (loss) by month analysis showing an unstable profitability trend.

Therefore, in this case, we cannot call victory yet. There is more work to be done.

In the next chapter, we will examine post-turnaround stabilization and control.

Chapter 31
Stabilization and Control

As previously stated, the long-term success of an operational turnaround depends on the execution of the post-turnaround stabilization, and on the implementation and fulfillment of a comprehensive control package.

Stabilization

After the vast and complex changes brought by an operational turnaround, a great deal of attention needs to be given to stabilization. Like any other goal we are working to achieve, stabilization needs to be defined, with milestones and measurable goals. Such an example could be achieving X amount of positive cash flow by end of year, being debt-free by end of next year, and restoring all lost market share in 24 months. As with any other company-wide goals, by engaging the XPeGoals methodology, we can align the organization and achieve the stabilization goals just as we have achieved the turnaround goals.

Stabilization has yet another dimension—one closer to the people side of the equation. Employees need to know when the restructuring has been completed, when they can breathe easier and drop the fear level down one notch. There is a continued need for two-way communication, recognizing effort and achievement on one side, and celebrating success on the other.

It is well worth the investment to put together communication material that shows in detail the actions that have been completed: quality gains, efficiencies, cost reduction, avoidance success stories, and all improvement work—completed and in progress. In most cases, it's also

worth it to restate the company vision, and communicate it thoroughly—whether modified during the turnaround or not.
Another key part of stabilization is to redefine a long-term strategy. After a few months of sudden, abundant change, the need for a long-term vision is quite obvious. The new long-term strategy will serve as the backbone for the recently turned-around business, driving cohesion around a common growth vision, engaging employees, and promoting stability.

Control Package

From many different points of view, since the downturn commenced, and during the turnaround, the business was the cliff diver holding his breath until he could resurface again. This holding of breath comes in many shapes and forms: added workload on existing employees, minimal maintenance to facilities and equipment, postponed upgrades in hardware and software, or lack of innovation programs. Therefore, a significant appetite to go wild and restore all these lost or suspended functions will surface, once we see a couple of months of profits. The business equivalent of the diver's gasp for air once he resurfaces, this tendency of resuming all "normal" spending patterns abruptly needs to be kept under control. To maintain control in an effective manner we need to follow a few steps.

Identifying Optimal Ranges

Document optimal parameters for each business function and unit, as uncovered during the turnaround. In many cases, we have pushed processes to their limits; therefore, documentation of these process capabilities and limits should be available as a reference. By examining these limits, documented levels of productivity, other metrics, and the relationships among them, we can find the optimal ranges for many such processes.

To illustrate, we will take an example from a manufacturing environment—more precisely, the fashion apparel company described in Chapter 21. We will be considering occupancy as the percentage of labor hours spent operating the sewing machine, and annualized turnover as the number of terminated employees per month (regrettable or not), divided by total number of employees, and multiplied by 12. Charted together and based on our measured and documented findings, we will notice that pushing occupancy too far will have an unwanted effect on employee retention.

This effect applies to voluntary turnover: employees burn out faster, get aches and pains from not being allowed to stretch and move around, they experience an overall stressful, unhappy environment, plus the fact that the labor market has less-demanding alternatives available. Involuntary turnover is also increased: the company is terminating the employees for low performance in an accelerated manner, because they cannot achieve and sustain a high occupancy rate.

Nevertheless, the cost of replacing a skilled employee is high, impacting both the operational budget and the product quality (new employee learning curve has a higher defect rate). So, despite the fact that we might want to push productivity through the ceiling, there is an optimal balance where we'd like to operate, as reflected in the chart below.

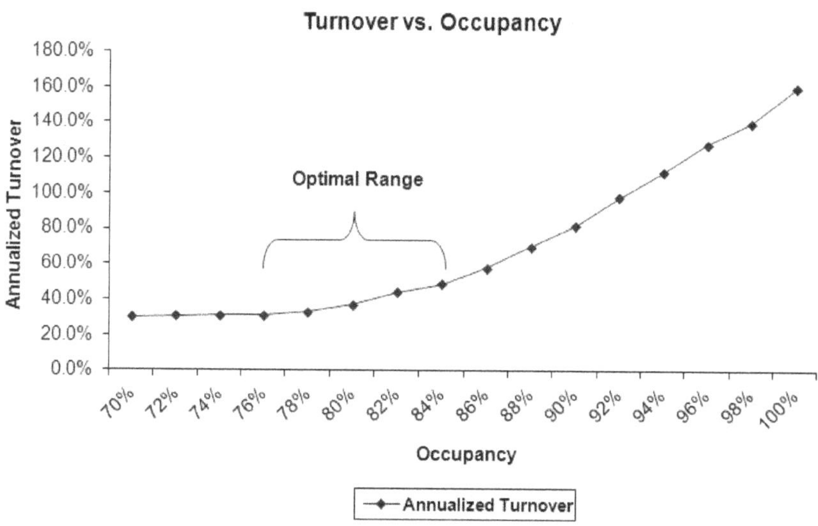

Fig. 31.1. Turnover vs. occupancy chart, showing optimal range.

The analysis tells us that we should not let occupancy drop under 76 percent —it would be wasteful, we would have an idle labor force, not effectively engaged in the manufacturing process. However, occupancy should not be pushed higher than 84 percent—beyond which turnover becomes a risk, with all the unwanted consequences. Therefore, our occupancy optimal range for this process is 78–84 percent.

Periodic Data Reviews—Dashboards

Once these optimal ranges are established, a daily–weekly–monthly mechanism of data capture and review can be set up. In conjunction with our XPeGoals matrix dashboards, we can easily track and see if any metric or process output falls outside the control range, while also keeping an eye on the results. This is mainly how we can ensure that we do not sacrifice something less visible while achieving our goals.

For example, if we would only be achieving our goals by pushing occupancy to 90 percent, it might take a while to see the negative effect of the high turnover; in the interim, we would have functioned with a less-than-desired global efficiency and effectiveness. In short, we need to ensure we do not develop tunnel vision around a goal, and fail to see and react to other interrelated areas of interest.

Avoid Repeating History

The defects that have caused the need of operational turnaround action are worth documenting and avoiding through control mechanisms. Those defects are the multitude of failure modes, incorrect parameters, inflexible processes, increased variability in processes, and overall culture. By documenting the positive changes we have made, combined with "red flag" values for parameters and action plans, we avoid repeating history by falling into the same error pattern.

An example of such a "red flag" value for a parameter can be in the case of turnover, as defined above, if it climbs higher than 50 percent annualized. An action plan could consist of an investigation into the causes of higher turnover, a pay level realignment with the market to ensure we are still competitive, etc.

Resist the Urge to Push a Stable, Efficient Process beyond the Limit

Except for carefully selected continuous improvement initiatives, ones that challenge some residual process inefficiencies, or help current processes keep up with the times (upgrades in technology and systems, channels of service, etc.), a stable and efficient process should be allowed to add value and yield results without constant challenges and change. After spending precious time and resources, we need to find the optimal ranges and a perfectly balanced approach among effectiveness, efficiency, quality, and customer and employee satisfaction. Just by ensuring we are steadily functioning within these optimal ranges will help to generate the stability we need for our future growth.

Chapter 32
Developing a Long-Term, Customer-Centric Strategy

There were numerous benefits derived from developing a customer-centric turnaround plan. Gathering and analyzing valuable voice-of-customer input throughout the process of restructuring ensured that we did not sacrifice, in any way, our customers' satisfaction or confidence with our product and service. Furthermore, by gaining customer intelligence we were able to steer our changes toward what makes a difference for the customer, both in purchasing decision making and also loyalty and customer retention. The same rules apply going forward, and the stabilization and return to growth strategy should be a customer-centric one, just as the operational turnaround was.

In Chapter 12, we were analyzing voice-of-customer feeds around deterrents to purchasing for an online music store, to help guide our decision making around going green and increasing sales. That analysis is charted in Fig. 32.1:

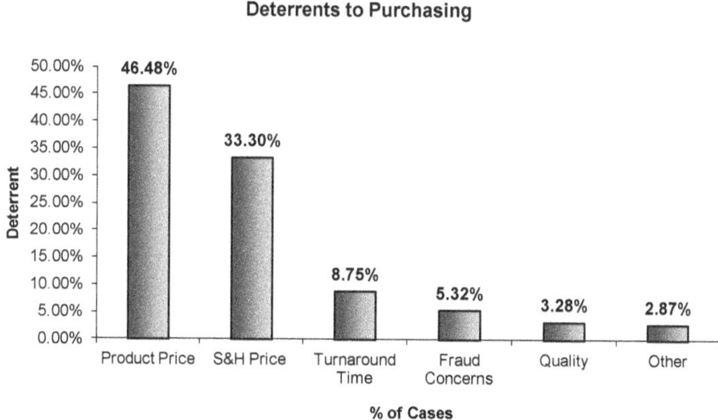

Fig. 32.1. Voice-of-customer (VOC) analysis of deterrents to purchasing.

Using the same methodology to capture voice of customer after the departure from the website without purchasing, we can start tracking both the impact of our action plans and trends for each deterrent, over time. For example, using the same action plan as designed in Chapter 12, a few months later we added PayPal as a payment option to address fraud concerns, and we have revised down our pricing in both products and shipping.

How do we know it is working? Quite simple . . . we continue the same process of surveying our online store customers who exit without purchasing, using the same survey methodology, unaltered, and we compare to our starting (or reference) point, which we are considering as a baseline. In parallel, we also want to keep an eye on the online store conversion rate, defined as the percentage of online store customers who exit the site after completing a transaction. Why is that? That is where it would show if the deterrent action plan is working overall. It would also allow for a normalized look at the survey data, because, in our deterrent analysis, we are showing percentages that sum up to 100 percent.

Therefore, if we improve all categories of deterrent, that would not be visible as an overall percentage of deterrent, because their weight of the total might not change. For example, two, illustrated as 20 percent of 10, is by far less than 20, illustrated as 20 percent of 100. In the absolute customer headcount value, we have dramatically improved from 20 deterred customers, down to 2 customers, while the percentage of total stayed the same—20 percent of all deterrents. The normalized view allows a better tracking of results. However, the "percentage of total deterrents" view is a useful tool in prioritizing action plans and watching solved categories lose priority or simply vanish.

Let's resume the analysis. After the completion of the initial action plan, here are the findings:

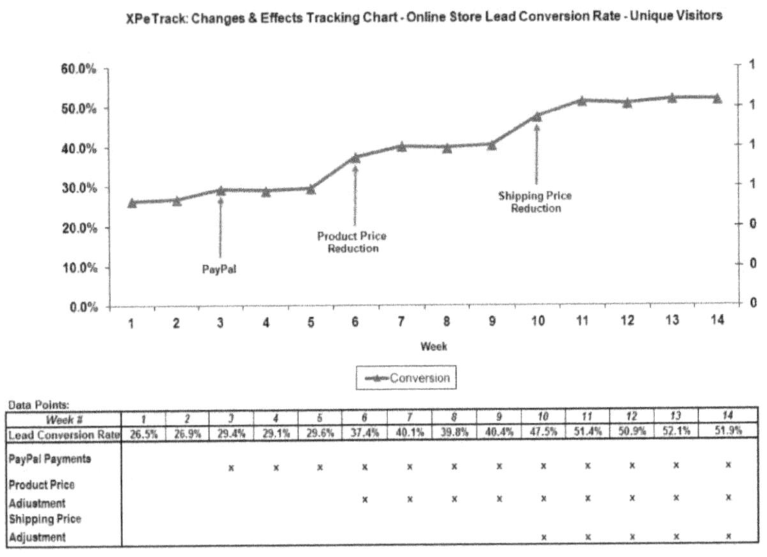

Week #	1	2	3	4	5	6	7	8	9	10	11	12	13	14
Lead Conversion Rate	26.5%	26.9%	29.4%	29.1%	29.6%	37.4%	40.1%	39.8%	40.4%	47.5%	51.4%	50.9%	52.1%	51.9%
PayPal Payments			x	x	x	x	x	x	x	x	x	x	x	x
Product Price Adiustment						x	x	x	x	x	x	x	x	x
Shipping Price Adjustment										x	x	x	x	x

Fig. 32.2. XPeTrack changes and effects—lead conversion rate for online channel .

Using XPeTrack, we are charting online store lead conversion, measuring unique visitors to avoid artificial dilution. XPeTrack reflects the positive effect of our action plan items in customers' decision to purchase.

How did the deterrents change after the action plan? Maintaining the same priority order as in the initial chart, we are noticing that fraud concerns have dropped significantly, to a negligible level. We are also noticing a newcomer—one that signals the fact that our product offering has fallen behind the customers' ever-evolving tastes and interests: selection.

Our online store doesn't have a wide—or updated—enough selection of titles; in short, our customers cannot find in our store what they are looking for. Product and shipping price are still high; lower than before, yet still high, indicating that our price adjustment actions might have not been deep enough. Finally, turnaround time seems to have gained momentum.

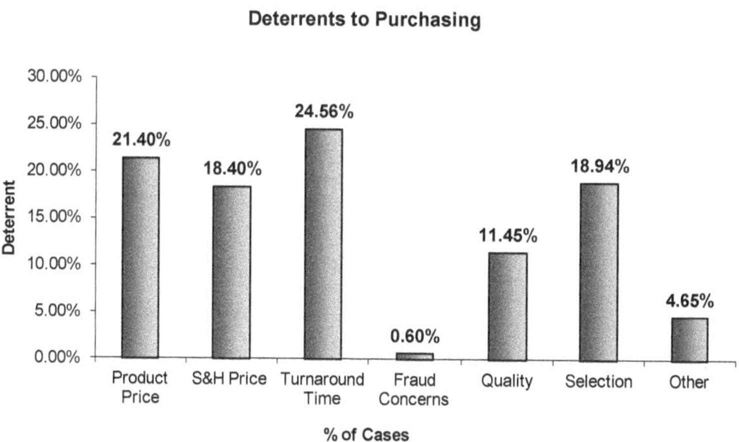

Fig. 32.3. Voice-of-customer (VOC) analysis of deterrents to purchasing, after the execution of the action plan.

Let's rearrange these bars, by order of magnitude, to allow prioritization of ongoing action plan:

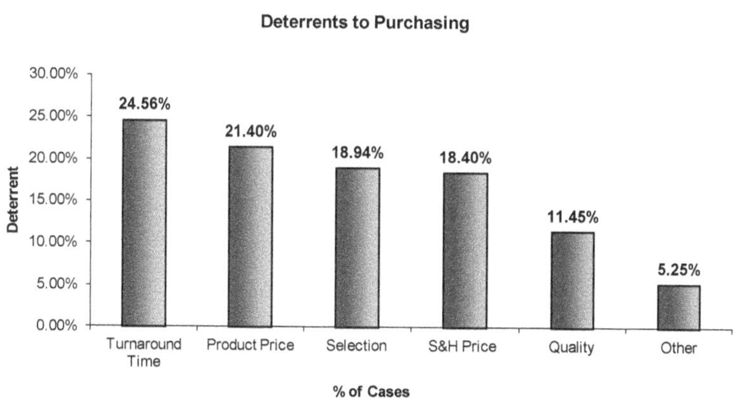

Fig. 32.4. Voice-of-customer (VOC) analysis of deterrents to purchasing, after the execution of the action plan—arranged in Pareto priority order.

"Fraud concerns" has been assimilated in "other," due to its now small size.

These two views of deterrents are not normalized; so we cannot really grasp the improvement made in any of the categories. Let's normalize the data around product price, to see the actual benefit.

Normalized Deterrent Analysis		
Unique Visitors	100,000	105,000
Timeline	Full Month Before Price Action	Full Month After Price Action
Total Deterred %	70.40%	60.02%
Total Deterred Net	70,400	63,021
Product Price Deterred %	46.48%	21.40%
Product Price Deterred Net	32,722	13,486

Fig. 32.5. Normalized deterrent analysis—before and after action plan.

We read this like a story. If, during the complete month before the product pricing action we had 100,000 unique visitors to our online store, and, out of those, 70.4 percent did not purchase, a net of 70,400 customers decided to leave without completing a transaction. Out of these, 46.48 percent were deterred by the price of our product; that is a net of 32,722 customers. After completing the product price reduction, we have seen that, out of a complete month's visitor count of 105,000, only 60.02 percent decided to leave without purchasing, representing a net count of 63,021 customers. Out of these, product pricing deterred 21.40 percent of them, amounting to a net of 13,486 customers.

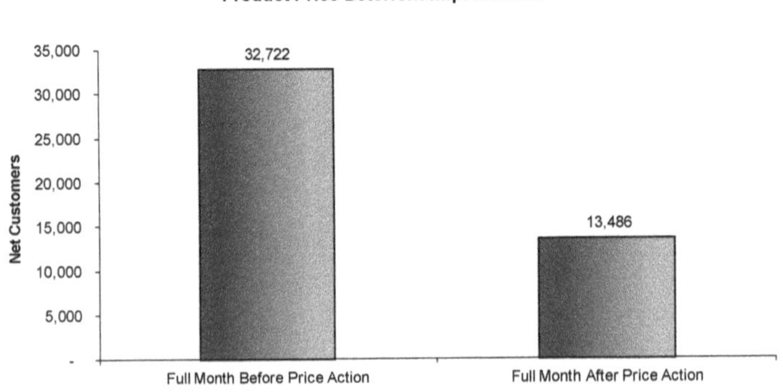

Fig. 32.6. Product price deterrent improvement.

Let's take the story further yet. We have seen a drop in net (normalized) product pricing deterred customers of 59 percent. Due to this pricing reduction, we have gained 19,235 more customers. If we multiply this number by the average purchasing price, we have the dollar value of the pricing drop benefit. If we take the cost of the action out (the balance of customers multiplied by the average drop in order value), we find the net benefit of the product pricing action, and we can decide if we can further drop pricing, as it is still among the top three deterrents to purchasing. XPeTrack for lead conversion combined with analysis of deterrents are the core components of what should become our customer-centric dashboard, with weekly and monthly reviews.

Drawing the conclusions from our example and applying them to the development of a long-term customer-centric strategy, three things are essential for its success.

Things Change and Evolve—Customer-Centric Process Improvement Never Ends

The process described above should never end. As we move ahead with improvements, our customers also evolve. In the example above, by surveying a few months later we find that we no longer satisfy with our selection. We also see that the turnaround time has the pole position as a deterrent. All this supports the idea that this type of customer-centric action should have a continued and supported role in our long-term strategy.

There are numerous examples of companies that have reached tremendous success, then gradually faded away because they did not create a long-term customer-centric strategy, one meant to ensure they keep in touch with their evolving customer. That would have also given them grounds to evolve. A strategy like that would have created the on-going basis for constant innovation.

Consider an NPS Strategy

A net promoter score (NPS) strategy can be designed and implemented in a similar manner, allowing us valuable insight into the growth potential of our business, especially in the consumer market. Just as with any customer intelligence program, NPS work is (almost) never done. Such efforts are compensated by the strong correlation between high NPS values and long-term business growth.

Chapter 33
Conclusion

All major endeavors, such as an operational turnaround, can be frightening at first, a challenge to execute, and rewarding in the end. Even after this exciting journey is over, we have a few things left to do.

Investigate and Document What Went Wrong

When there is enough time to do such work, but not too late after the fact, an important step in preventing future hardship is to investigate, pinpoint, and document what were the root causes of the financial crisis. In some cases, it could be an aggressive expansion plan. Alternatively, it could well be over-confident, decision making that favored fixed-cost structures, such as real estate development or unusually long-term leases.

In other cases, the company culture goes wrong and pulls everything down with it. In any case, such findings are instrumental in creating failsafe standard operating procedures to prevent future distress. For example, having a "positive ROI within 12 months" decision-making criterion for all expenses exceeding $10,000 could be helpful in avoiding corporate impulse shopping—insufficiently researched investments, "gut-feel" or "feel-good" purchases, or "strategically important" investments that are out of alignment with the company's strategic goals.

Keep Your Consultant on Speed Dial for a While

Your operational turnaround consultant was able to find and fix the issues behind the financial hardship of the company. He can do it again, any time, and it is going to be much easier than last time. Therefore, it may well be worth his time and your money to keep him on speed dial for a while—double-check about major decisions or investments, for example.

Follow-Up Contracts

Along the same line as above, your operational turnaround consultant should be invited to execute a number of follow-up contracts, with a focus on stabilization, post-stabilization milestones, and future growth. He can take temperature readings now and then, collect and analyze some voice of employees on a periodic basis. All this—just to make sure things are kept on a smooth sailing path, and that the company does not fall back into previous negative behaviors.

Set Post-Stabilization Milestones

For the progressive, innovative, customer-centric company, finalizing a turnaround is not an end—it is a beginning. Developing an ambitious strategic plan, setting post-stabilization milestones, and executing this plan with the same rigor as we have executed the turnaround plan will ensure the relentless progress of our business that will demonstrate success beyond the wildest expectations. The only way from here is up, and the sky is the limit.

In conclusion, no matter how desperate the situation might seem, if you have resolve, dedication, undeterred willingness to succeed, and a good operational turnaround team, you can make it happen.

About the Author

Jack Skinner is a seasoned business leader with an engaging writing style, presenting detailed case studies, how-tos, and diagrams that allow readers to implement the featured methodologies with significant ease.

Far from being a conventional theoretician, Skinner's hands-on business experience comes across in practical, tested methodologies and flexible, direct, to-the-point approaches for the most daunting challenges of customer centric business transformation.

Bibliography

Bibeault, D. B. (1998). *Corporate Turnaround: How Managers Turn Losers into Winners!* New York: McGraw-Hill.

Gary, L. (2001). For *Whom the Bell Curve Tolls—The Controversial Practice of Forced Ranking.* Boston: Harvard Business School.

Lencioni, P. M. (2004). *Death by Meeting: A Leadership Fable . . . About Solving the Most Painful Problem in Business.* San Francisco: Jossey-Bass.

Lipman-Blumen, J., Drucker, P. F., and Ito, M. (2006) "Toxic Leadership" (Article published by Graduate School of Management—Claremont Graduate University).

McDonald, L. G. and Robinson, P. (2009). *A Colossal Failure of Common Sense: The Inside Story of the Collapse of Lehman Brothers.* New York: Crown Publishing Group.

Menkes, J. (2006). *Executive Intelligence: What All Great Leaders Have.* New York: HarperCollins.

Owen, R. and Brooks, L. L. (2008) *Answering the Ultimate Question: How Net Promoter Can Transform Your Business.* San Francisco: Jossey-Bass.

Pyzdek, T. (2003). *The Six Sigma Handbook: The Complete Guide for Greenbelts, Blackbelts, and Managers at All Levels.* Revised and Expanded Edition. New York: McGraw-Hill.

Rosenbluth, H. and McFerrin Peters, D. (2002). *The Customer Comes*

Second: Put Your People First and Watch 'Em Kick Butt. New York: HarperCollins.

Sutton, G. (2001). *The Six-Month Fix: Adventures in Rescuing Failing Companies.* New York: Wiley.

www.ingramcontent.com/pod-product-compliance
Lightning Source LLC
Chambersburg PA
CBHW020201200326
41521CB00005BA/206

* 9 7 8 1 9 4 5 3 0 2 1 7 6 *